CHURCH ACCOUNTING METHODS

CHURCH BUSINESS MANAGEMENT SERIES

CHURCH
ACCOUNTING
METHODS

Arthur L. Walker

PRENTICE-HALL, INC.
Englewood Cliffs, New Jersey

Library of Congress Catalog Card Number: 63-18109

Printed in the United States of America. T 13372

PRENTICE-HALL INTERNATIONAL, INC., *London*
PRENTICE-HALL OF AUSTRALIA, PTY., LTD., *Sydney*
PRENTICE-HALL OF CANADA, LTD., *Toronto*
PRENTICE-HALL OF INDIA (PRIVATE) LTD., *New Delhi*
PRENTICE-HALL OF JAPAN, INC., *Tokyo*
PRENTICE-HALL DE MEXICO, S.A., *Mexico City*

EDITOR'S INTRODUCTION

THE SERIES of books in which this volume is included was prepared for all who seek new insight and specific guidance in administering business affairs of churches. These books represent the most comprehensive publishing project ever completed in the field of church business management.

Each book in the series is based on two major premises: First, if churches are to accomplish their purposes effectively, their business affairs must be managed as well as, or better than, those of other organizations. Second, since churches are service-rendering rather than profit-making, and because of their voluntary nature and the trustee relationship involved, their business policies and practices must differ in certain respects from those of commercial enterprises and the differences must be clearly identified and thoroughly understood.

These books are intended (1) to help clergy and laity develop additional competence for effective stewardship of church business responsibilities, (2) to provide stimulation and practical suggestions for professional career employment as business managers of churches and related non-profit organizations, and (3) to make available an educational basis for strengthening the role of pastors as chief administrators of individual churches.

5

In planning, organizing, and evaluating this series of books the editor was confronted with certain basic questions to which explicit answers had not been published. What *is* church business management? What is it *for?* What is it *not?* What is it *not for?* What are its boundaries? The following tentative definition by the editor is the result of his pioneer effort to delineate and identify this field:

Church Business Management is the science and art of administering church program development, financial resources, physical facilities, office services, staff personnel, and public relations, all in accordance with the most effective standards of religious stewardship. Included in this concept are such managerial processes as forecasting, planning, organizing, delegating, controlling, evaluating, and reporting. Management of a church's business responsibilities is a facilitating function to be regarded not as an end in itself but as an important means to a worthy end.

Illustrations of what may be considered "church business management" have come from congregations that have added a professional business manager to the employed staff. A carefully written job description for such a staff member usually can help any church identify the business functions that are essential in establishing and attaining its distinctive purposes. Such job descriptions should, and often do, represent the business manager as a professional consultant and resource leader in helping church officers and staff, both volunteers and employees, perform their administrative duties in relation to the ministry of:

1. *Program Development*—planning, organizing, and scheduling all appropriate means available to the church for achieving its objectives and goals.
2. *Financial Management*—budgeting, obtaining, safeguarding, disbursing, and accounting for all financial resources.
3. *Property Management*—using, maintaining, and acquiring

physical facilities such as buildings and grounds, furniture, and equipment.

4. *Office Management*—providing systematic programs of scheduling, communicating, and recording services to facilitate achievement of administrative functions.

5. *Personnel Management*—determining and describing staff positions; enlisting, assigning, and training nonprofessional staff, both volunteers and employees; developing and maintaining staff morale.

6. *Public Relations*—communicating the church's concept of its purposes, its programs, its accomplishments, its potentialities, and its needs.

Church business management as viewed in this light, and when applied creatively through proper use of collaborative and democratic procedures, is a significant phase of a meaningful spiritual ministry. How successfully and effectively the author of each book in this series has amplified the foregoing philosophy and specifications each reader will, of course, judge for himself.

For invaluable advice and practical assistance on various phases of this endeavor the editor is grateful to Dr. Nathan A. Baily, Dean of the School of Business Administration, The American University. Dean Baily's keen interest in this field and his able leadership in establishing the American University Center for Church Business Management were significant factors in the development of this series of books.

Clyde W. Humphrey
General Editor

Washington, D. C.

PREFACE

THIS HANDBOOK is addressed to all those persons who are concerned with making and maintaining financial records for churches and their related organizations. Its purpose is to serve as a guide to those who design and keep a well-ordered system of financial accounts for churches.

The content of the book is arranged in logical sequence so that those who have had little or no formal training in church accounting may become reasonably proficient through careful and patient study of the text and the illustrations that accompany the discussions.

The author has combined many years of professional accounting experience and college teaching to produce a manual of procedures that will be helpful as a study guide for those who desire to pursue a program of self-instruction, or as a member of a study group. Church bookkeepers, financial secretaries, business managers, treasurers, ministers, and various committeemen will find in this manual a source of profitable reading and study. Much of the material is applicable to smaller churches as well as to the larger ones, and for all denominations, although many of the forms, terminology, and examples are admittedly drawn from the Methodist Church. Each chapter is introduced by a series of overview questions and problems that will serve as guidelines for study.

We present this handbook in the hope that it may be a ready source of useful information and give direction to all persons who have responsibility for keeping records of financial stewardship. Our reasons for producing this volume are summarized in the Major Premises that follow:

1. If churches are to carry out their total program effectively, their economic affairs must be managed as competently as those of successful commercial businesses.

2. Because churches are service-producing rather than profit-making institutions, their accounting procedures will differ in some respects from those of commercial businesses, and these differences can be identified.

3. Periodic accounting to membership for their individual gifts on a regular schedule is a service of primary consideration and a responsibility of church business management.

4. Accounting for *all* church receipts and expenditures in a businesslike manner is a basic function of church business management.

5. Churches have both the opportunities and responsibilities for setting examples of ethical practices in business management in the community.

Much of the inspiration and motivation for attempting this handbook came from fellow-members of the several Seminars and Institutes on Church Management conducted at The Center for Church Business Management, School of Business Administration of The American University, Washington, D. C., 1961-62. In particular, the Rev. Clyde W. Humphrey, under whose capable leadership these seminars were held, is due a large measure of credit for those features of this book that may have real value.

I am deeply indebted also to many other persons and organizations for their friendly and helpful assistance in supplying ideas, proven practices, procedures, and constructive criticisms that were so essential in the production of this volume. To all these and other friends whose wise counsel and quiet patience helped to make this effort more enjoyable and worthwhile, I extend my sincere thanks.

Arthur L. Walker

CONTENTS

LIST OF ILLUSTRATIONS

Chapter 1

THE PURPOSES OF
CHURCH ACCOUNTING

What is the nature of an "account"?

How can accurate and systematic financial records contribute to effective individual and group stewardship?

How can accounting methods assist church management officials in planning for progress?

What qualities of Christian stewardship are exemplified in effective keeping of church accounts?

These questions indicate the points of principal concern in this chapter. You should be able to make complete and intelligent answers to these and other related problems upon completion of your reading and study of the next few pages.

THE NATURE OF ACCOUNTS

An account is a simple and convenient device for indicating visually the increases (+) or decreases (−) resulting from an exchange of values in a business transaction. The nature of an account is readily understood when compared to the apothecary balances or to a teeter-totter, or to a see-saw. The two opposite sides are in perfect equilibrium when no weights (values) are placed on either side, and also when equal weights (values) are placed on either side of the fulcrum. The diagrams below will demonstrate both conditions.

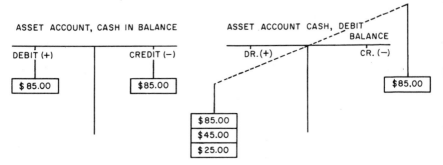

Illustration 1. Debit Balance Accounts

Assets are things or values owned, such as *cash, buildings, furniture*, and *stock certificates*. Each asset or group of assets, such as office equipment, is set up in a separate account. Additions or increases to assets are recorded on the left, or debit, side of the account. Subtractions or decreases are recorded on the right, or credit, side of the account. Therefore, asset accounts are debited for all increases (+) and credited for all decreases (−). Accounts are said to be "in balance" when the total debits and total credits are equal. All asset accounts normally have a debit balance. Cost and expense accounts such as *rent, office supplies, utilities,* and *salaries* also have debit balances.

Liability and income accounts are debited for decreases (−) and credited for increases (+), the reverse of the rule for assets and expense. Liabilities are values *owed*, or obligations to be paid at a future time, such as *notes* or *mortgages payable, taxes payable,* and *accounts payable*. Generally, there is a separate account in the ledger for each liability and each income item. Examples of income accounts are *current envelopes, plate offering, special gifts, com-*

munion offerings, and *rents* from *leased property.* Liability and income accounts normally show a credit balance, indicated in the diagrams below.

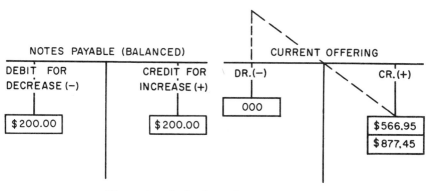

Illustration 2. Credit Balance Accounts

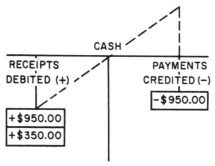

Illustration 3. The Cash Account with Debit Balance of $350.00

Obviously, the account for CASH could not show a credit balance without being overdrawn. The debit or (+) side of all asset accounts—things owned—normally have an excess of values over the credit or (−) side of the account. The same principle holds true for all cost and expense accounts such as salaries, rent, and utilities. Conversely, all liability accounts such as notes payable, accounts payable, and FICA (Federal Insurance Contributions Act) taxes due will normally show a credit balance that reflect the obligation. All income accounts abide by this same principle, as, for example, receipts from pledges or contributions, special gifts, plate offerings, and miscellaneous receipts.

PURPOSES OF CHURCH ACCOUNTING

Church accounting has three primary purposes: (1) to furnish complete, accurate, orderly and timely financial information to church fiscal agents necessary for the proper handling of receipts and expenditures; (2) to provide the official body of the church the records and reports needed for planning and budgeting the resources of the congregation; and (3) to keep individual members currently informed on the status of their financial stewardship commitment.

THE METHOD

Accounts are kept in a book called the *ledger,* which is a book of *final entry.* The results of transactions are generally *posted* or copied to the ledger accounts from books of *original entry* known as *journals.* Back of the journal entries are the documents, checks, receipts, sales tickets, cash and various evidences of transfer of values from one person or organization to another.

Under some circumstances, records of transactions may be entered directly into the ledger account, but almost always at the expense of explanatory information sufficient for intelligible interpretation. In other instances, entries are made simultaneously in the appropriate journal and in the ledger by means of a "one-time" writing system.

The usual or traditional format of the ledger account is similar to the capital "T", with identical sides for writing the date, explanation, reference page number or ledger

(LF) folio, and ruled columns for the amount of value or money. This is commonly called the "Standard Ledger Form," as shown in Illustration 4.

1963 DATE		ITEMS	FOL.	✓	DEBITS	1963 DATE		ITEMS	FOL.	✓	CREDITS
Feb.	1	Offering	301		954 25	Feb.	15	Salaries	411		425 00
	4	Pledges Pd.	301		464 30		15	Car Allow.	411.1		50 00

ACCOUNT NO. *101* NAME *Cash* SHEET NO. _____
ADDRESS TERMS RATING CREDIT LIMIT

Illustration 4. Standard Ledger Form

Another form of the ledger is one that provides three money columns grouped on the right side of the page, including a special column for recording the current balance after each entry, as shown in Illustration 5.

Illustration 5. Balance Ledger Form

DATE		ITEMS	FOL.	✓	DEBITS	CREDITS	BALANCE
Feb.	1	Current Offering - Plate	301		954 25		954 25
	4	Current Offering - Mail	301		464 30		1418 55
	15	Salary of Pastor	411			425 00	993 55
	15	Car Allowance	411.1			50 00	943 55

NAME *Cash*   *101*   ADDRESS
1963   BUSINESS   INDIVIDUAL   TERMS   CREDIT LIMIT   RATING

ACCOUNTING PROMOTES STEWARDSHIP

The accounting system must serve the interests and needs of all members and all segments of the church. The individual member should be in a position to know, at frequent intervals, and upon request, the extent to which he has met his financial stewardship commitments. Through such provisions, not only will the morale of the individual and that of the collective membership be maintained at a relatively higher level, but the rate of support will be motivated due to confidence born of businesslike procedure.

For the business manager, or for the financial secretary, the system of accounts must reveal at all times and without the necessity of laborious compiling, classifying, and summarizing, the relationship of the operating accounts to projections made in budget estimates for receipts and expenditures.

A good accounting system serves as a periodic reminder to the entire church body of the mission and continuing purposes for which the church exists. It is human nature to forget some of those things one ought to do. Often, commitments made in good faith and with high purpose fail because of lapse of memory and fading enthusiasm that were quite vivid at the time of the original decision. Thus, it is not only desirable but necessary to find an effective means of helping people to "remember" their good intentions, and of their responsibilities "to do those things they ought to do."

A good system of accounts is tailored to meet the needs for reporting the sources of income and expenditures for a given period of operation. The good system is also simple and easy to use and is readily summarized in reports. The size of the church will dictate to a very large extent some of the features of the accounting plan. The system must fit the church whether large or small, being neither too simple for a complex situation nor too involved for a simple need.

A church with an annual budget of $50,000 or less may be adequately served with little more than a Multicolumnar Cash Journal and individual subscriber's card file. If the number of operating accounts is few and the need for entries infrequent, all posting and reporting can be done efficiently and economically by manual methods.

The accounting system serves as a basis for budgetary administration. As we shall learn, the budget is a planned program of receipts and expenditures for a specified time, generally a year. Only by keeping a systematic record of income and expenditures can the governing body or a designated church official determine whether the rate of income and expenditure is working out at or near the projections made in the planned budget. If, for example, the amount estimated for property maintenance is $4,300 for the year, or $358.33 a month, and the second quarterly report shows a total expenditure of $2,800, an additional appropriation must be made, or a curtailment of maintenance expenditures will be necessary in the last half of the year. It is generally desirable to show at least once a month the progress of income and expenditures for every line item in the operating budget. The following specimen (Illustration 6) indicates the meaning and value of this type of progress report. Note however that more than one expense item is included in a single listing, which violates good accounting practice.#

The practice of employing automated machine and electronic processes for handling the huge volume of data in large churches in becoming increasingly common. Not only is it uneconomical to use manual methods in such situations, but the task of producing completely current financial statements for individual subscribers and for management becomes more difficult. As the volume of recording and reporting increases, the advisability of employing data-handling equipment within the church office, or contracting for accounting services outside, becomes more advisable.

Spring Hill Church

Report on General Operating Fund Expenditures
Month Ending October 31, 1963

	1 Annual Budget	2 Monthly Budget	3 Spent for Month	4 Budgeted to Date	5 Spent to Date	6 Reserve, or Deficit*
Administrative Salaries	12,000.00	1,000.00	1,000.00	5,000.00	5,000.00	00.00
District Apportionment:						
Salary & Parsonage	585.00	48.75		293.55	195.00	98.55
District Work	935.00	77.91		389.55	311.72	77.83
Maint. Church Property	4,300.00	358.33	5.00	1,791.65	348.54	1,443.11
Welfare	1,200.00	100.00	92.90	500.00	581.26	81.26*
Fuel and Utilities	4,250.00	354.16	145.87	1,770.80	1,190.74	580.06
Prtg., Publ'ty & Office Sup.#	5,100.00	425.00	276.12	2,125.00	1,614.94	510.06
Janitors' Supplies	375.00	31.25	7.60	156.25	211.28	55.03*
Pulpit Supply	100.00	8.33		41.65	30.00	11.65
Insurance	1,800.00	150.00	231.28	750.00	241.28	508.72
Religious Education	1,600.00	133.33	150.64	666.66	488.85	177.81
Miscellaneous	3,600.00	300.00	344.72	1,500.00	1,561.79	61.79*
Auto—Rental Allowances	4,050.00	337.49	337.49	1,687.45	1,687.45	00.00
Benevolences	9,000.00	750.00	875.00	3,750.00	3,800.00	50.00*
Totals	$96,000.00	8,000.00	7,620.00	40,000.00	38,345.20	1,654.80

Note
* Overspent budget, prorated basis to date.

Illustration 6. Monthly Statement of Budget Progress

CHURCH ACCOUNTING IS MORE THAN FINANCIAL RECKONING

Church accounting in its fullest sense suggests not only the faithful and accurate keeping of financial records, but also includes a keen awareness of the necessity of maintaining records of the human resources—interests, talents, and motivations—of every member of the congregation. For example, a member who possesses musical or artistic talent, or the ability to teach, or the capacity for group leadership, or the ability to direct auxiliary functions, may very well have values to the church program far in excess of one who tithes even thousands of dollars in cash.

A good accounting system will provide means for determining these human resources and give force and direction to them to the fullest possible development of the member himself and to the glory of God. Every member has a potential resource for the progress of the church. Failure to find and assess these dormant or unexpressed talents and to develop them to their highest potential is a gross failure for the church leadership and, indeed, for the whole church program. Those who serve most, grow most! Conversely, those who grow most, serve better!

A SACRED TRUST

Anyone who is honored with the keeping of church accounts truly has a sacred trust. The manner in which the work is done bespeaks the quality of his stewardship. Neat and accurate records inspire a sense of pride and indicate an attitude of reverence. On the other hand, sloppy and inaccurate work denotes a low level of dedication and a dismal misconception of the Christian stewardship inherent in church accounting. This is a task to challenge one's best efforts and most creative abilities. The good steward continually strives to so design the system that it will be a tailor-made fit for his accounting needs. The best system in all its details of design and operational procedures will evolve only after a period of patient and devoted effort. Truly, there is an unmistakable quality of stewardship in keeping the accounts, as well as in presiding over the official board. The Psalmist said, "I had rather be a doorkeeper in the house of my God, than to dwell in the tents of wickedness" (Psalm 84:10). Quality of stewardship is not to be measured by the rank of officialdom.

Chapter 2

TYPES OF
ACCOUNTING SYSTEMS

What are the limitations of "single entry" bookkeeping?

What are the features of the "double entry" system?

What is a voucher system and how is it used?

HOW MUCH ACCOUNTING?

The number and kinds of books of accounts, memoranda, and summaries of financial data will be very largely determined by the size and the complexity of the annual budget. Any church may be "overorganized" or "underorganized" with respect to its records system. A good rule is to maintain only the records needed for the information required for periodic reports. An equally important objective is to achieve maximum simplicity consistent with the need for reports. The need for reports is implicit in the nature of the financial and human resource programs of the church. The greater the activity, the greater the need will be for reflecting the operation of these activities in the accounting system.

SINGLE ENTRY

The so-called *single entry system* is really not a system, because it lacks the elements of classification and organization of data that characterize the concept of "system." The single entry method of recording transactions is a simple listing of the events in the order of their happening, without recognizing the dual and simultaneous effect of producing a debit in one account while producing a corresponding credit in another.

One may keep a very exact record of all monies received, and all monies paid out, in a *daybook,* in strict chronological order with appropriate explanation. But at the end of the week, or the month, or the quarter, or the year, these memoranda will reveal only disconnectedly, even though correctly, the facts surrounding the various transactions. There will be considerable difficulty in determining how much was received from any particular source, or charged to any particular expense activity. While the record is simple and easily made, one cannot determine summarized information for periodic reports except by laborious and time-consuming effort. Only after a long period of painstakingly "picking out" receipts and expenditures for such items as offerings, contributions, salaries, benevolences, building maintenance, supplies, and other classes of financial activity, can a summary statement be made.

We learned in Chapter 1 that *two* accounts are always affected by every transaction. The daybook type of memorandum reflects the effect of the transaction on only one account. Hence, the term "single entry." Since there is no equivalent recorded credit for every debit, there is no easy way of proving the accuracy of the records by comparing the total debits with the total credits. Observe the difficulty in determining the total expenditures for office supplies in the following day-book record.

Although this may be an accurate record of transactions, the difficulty in summarizing the information can readily be seen by attempting to find the balance of cash on hand, assuming a beginning balance of $823.92 on December 31. Imagine the time consumed at the end of a month, or a

Cash Received & Paid

	January 1963	Description	CK. No.	Amount
1	1	Balance brought forward		$23.92
2	1	Pastor's salary, Dec. 1962	64	500.00
3	1	Tax on Salary Reserve (33.70)		
4	1	Offering for First Sunday		$42.62
5	2	Postage		20.00
6	3	Paid December Phone bill	65	1.68
7	3	Wednesday Offering	66	36.80
8	3	Repairs to Mimeograph		7.50
9	4	Groceries for Family night dinner	67	26.98
10	6	Collection from Family night dinner	68	$22.25
11	6	Kitchen help paid in cash		14.00
12	8	Bought food for needy family	69	7.50
13	8	Offering for Second Sunday		6.45
14	9	Paid Water & lights for December	70	28.42
15	10	Collection by mail		74.85
16	10	Paid for Printing Church Bulletin for Dec.	71	60.00
17	10	Bought Sheet Music - A.B. Monte Co.	72	1.20
18				
19				
20				
21				
22				
23				

Illustration 7. Single Entry Record

Illustration 8. Example of Double Entry

Cash Received and Paid

1963 Jan.	Explanation	LF CK	Dr.	Cr.	
1	Balance brought forward	✓	$123 92		1
	Pastor's salary			500 00	2
	Opening, First Sunday				3
2	Postage	64	74 262	200 0	4
3	Paid December phone bill	65		18 60	5
	Wednesday offering	66	36 80		6
	Repaired to Missionary	67		7 50	7
4	Groceries for Family Night dinner	68	42 25	269 ?	8
6	Collection School / Family Night dinner				9
	Kitchen supplies paid in cash			14 00	10
8	Bought food for needy family	69		7 50	11
	Offering, Second Sunday		614 15		12
9	Paid water + lights for Dec.	70		25 42	13
10	Collection by mail		74 65		14
	Paid for printing Bulletin	71		200 00	15
	Bought sheet music	72		12 90	16
					17
					18
					19
					20
					21
					22
					23

quarter, or a year, in stating the total cash received and expended and the total expended for utilities or any other item of expense. Observe the difficulty that you experience in quickly answering the following questions from the information in the record above.

(1) How much cash was received for the 10-day period?
(2) How much money was paid out?
(3) What is the current balance?
(4) How much more money was received for the family night dinner than was paid out for food and kitchen help?
(5) How much is due the Federal Government for taxes withheld?

Now observe the ease with which the totals for each income and expense account can be determined when the items are properly entered into a special columnar journal. Of course, not every account will have a column, but Illustration 8 demonstrates the principle of recording each item of receipts and expenditures in an appropriate account column.

Now refer to the previous questions and find the answers in the multicolumnar journal. It is very clear that the automatic classification provided by the columnar arrangement and the convenient "Dr." and "Cr." designations makes the task of summarizing quite simple.

VOUCHER SYSTEM

Some churches use a method of handling cash payments generally referred to as the *voucher system*. The primary advantage of this system is its control over expenditures by means of requiring written authorization for every cash disbursement. For example, to some official other than the bookkeeper or the cashier is delegated the responsibility of authorizing the issuance of all checks. The authority may be simply an initialing of an invoice or other acceptable memorandum of indebtedness. But behind every check there is an original and descriptive voucher or document establishing the validity of the payment.

For a permanent record of vouchers payable, a *Voucher Register* (Illustration 10) is maintained, with columns for:

(1) Account Dr.
(2) Date
(3) Voucher No.
(4) Payee
(5) Account Cr.
(6) Voucher Payable Cr.
(7) Disposition

Vouchers are numbered serially and upon approval are attached to the invoice to which they apply. The account title, Column 4, provides for crediting the account at the time of recording the liability and debiting it for the payment. Thus the difference between the "Dr." and "Cr." sides indicate at all times the amount of outstanding accounts payable.

Some variation of the voucher method of controlling expenditures is particularly applicable in churches that do not employ a full-time business manager or purchasing agent. Of course, the system is used also by business managers and purchasing agents. In all instances, the treasurer signs only those checks that are supported by an approved invoice or special voucher descriptive of merchandise delivered or services rendered. Statements of account without description of values received are not accepted for payment.

After the vouchers have been recorded in the "Voucher Register," they may be filed alphabetically in an "Unpaid Vouchers" file or filed numerically according to due date. When filed according to "Date Due," the folder or jacket becomes a tickler file and tends to prevent accounts payable from becoming overdue.

When an invoice or other document representing an obligation has been approved by signature or initial, it is said to have been "vouched" or authorized for payment. The approval may be written directly on the document or on a special form attached to the original paper. When a special form is used, it is filled in with the number of the invoice and a description of its contents, such as the specimen shown below. The primary purpose of "vouching" for payment is to place a responsible official in control over cash expenditures.

PURCHASES REQUISITION

Spring Hill Church
Anytown, U. S. A.

No. 101   Date 2/16/63

Quantity	Description
4 quires	Acme Mimeograph Stencils
6 reams	18# Mimeograph Bond

Date Ordered 2/17/63   Purpose or Use Office
Date Wanted 2/25/63   Date Delivered
Vendor Luck Stationery Company   Invoice No.
Account Charged Office Supplies   Approved by J.C.B.

Illustration 9. Purchases Requisition

The use of a special form, such as the "Purchases requisition," fixes the responsibility for placing orders for goods and services and attesting to their delivery. When the goods have been delivered and quantity and specifications verified, the receiving clerk completes the form and attaches it to the invoice in preparation for "approval," presumably by "J.C.B.," since he authorized the purchase. In the meantime, the bookkeeper may make the entry in the Voucher Register if such a record is maintained. See Illustration 10 (next page).

VOUCHER REGISTER FOR THE MONTH OF ___May___ 1963

1		2	3	4	5			6	7	
Sundry Accts. Dr.					Sundry Accts. Cr.			Vouchers Payable Cr.	Disposition	
Acct. No.	Amount	Day	Vchr. No.	TO WHOM ISSUED	Acct. No.	Amount	v		Date	Ck. No.
446	17 00	1	101	The Office Supply Co.	446			17 00		
442	187 50	2	102	Scott & Scott Co.	442			187 50	1/9/63	87
445	52 10	4	103	City Printing Co.	445			84 55		

Illustration 10. Vouchers Payable Register

Some churches use the "voucher check" similar to the example below, which provides sufficient space to describe in detail the purpose for which the payment is made. It has the added advantage of supplying a record for tax purposes for the payee.

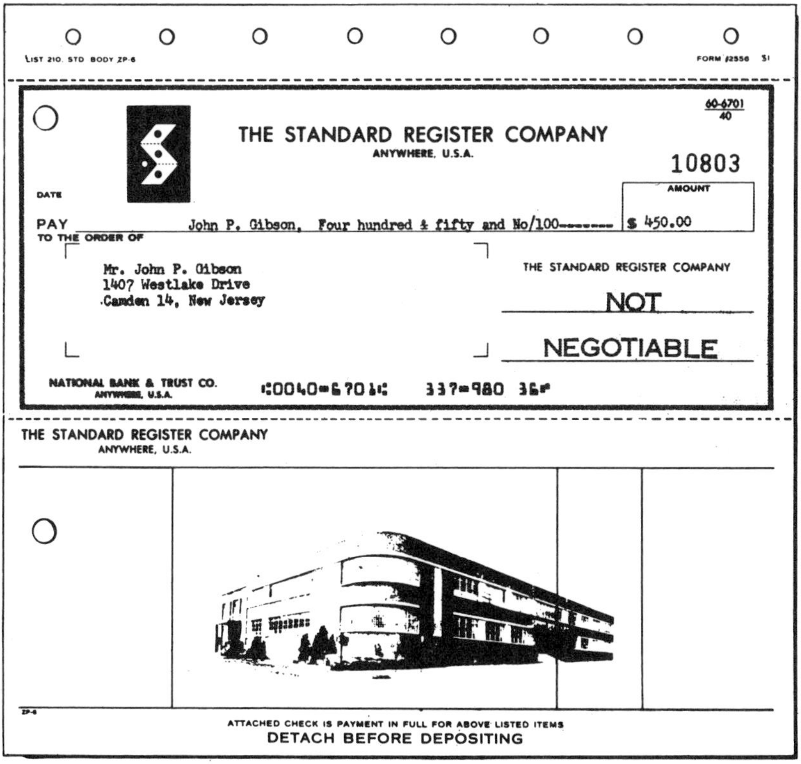

LIST 210. STD BODY ZP-6 FORM #2556 51

60-6701
40

THE STANDARD REGISTER COMPANY
ANYWHERE, U.S.A.

10803

DATE

AMOUNT

PAY TO THE ORDER OF John P. Gibson, Four hundred & fifty and No/100------- $ 450.00

Mr. John P. Gibson
1407 Westlake Drive
Camden 14, New Jersey

THE STANDARD REGISTER COMPANY

NOT NEGOTIABLE

NATIONAL BANK & TRUST CO.
ANYWHERE, U.S.A.

:0040-6701: 337-980 36

THE STANDARD REGISTER COMPANY
ANYWHERE, U.S.A.

ZP-6

ATTACHED CHECK IS PAYMENT IN FULL FOR ABOVE LISTED ITEMS
DETACH BEFORE DEPOSITING

Illustration 11. Voucher Check

PETTY CASH

Expenditures from the *petty cash* fund may be subject to voucher approval if the amount is consequential. Good practice sanctions the keeping of a journal record of miscellaneous expenditures, such as 65¢ for car fare, and presenting the memorandums and petty cash record to the treasurer at the time a check is requested to replenish the petty cash fund. It is understandable that some treasurers refuse to issue checks for any type of expenditure without supporting records that have been approved by the appropriate official. This practice is especially recommended in situations where several committee chairmen or other officials have the authority to issue purchase orders or to contract for services within their sphere of activity.

Everyone in charge of a petty cash fund should maintain a memorandum of petty cash expenditures, in a separate book, or as a section of one of the journals. This does not obviate the need for keeping in chronological order receipts and notations for each expenditure, regardless of how small they are.

Chapter 3

ACCOUNTING FOR WHAT
AND TO WHOM?

What church resources are included in the accounting procedures?

Who should receive summary reports on status of assets, liabilities, and needs?

How may individual members be informed of the status of their stewardship commitments?

SCOPE OF CHURCH ACCOUNTING

Both the scope and the nature of the accounting functions will vary from church to church within most denominations and, more particularly, from one type of church organization to another. Generally speaking, however, there is likely to be greater individuality in the congregational type of church than in those of connectional denominations.

The kind of reporting required by districts, synods, and dioceses exert strong influence on the types of accounts and the manner in which they are kept. In fact, in some church groups, the system may be very largely prescribed and the books and forms may be furnished by denominational headquarters. In such instances, the latitude for local innovations is restricted. A "standard" system and uniform procedures makes for uniformity and consistency of reporting, thereby making possible statistical comparisons of one group or locality with another. Also, the tabulation of aggregate data for large geographical areas is more easily accomplished. Without some consistency among units, it may be difficult to assemble data on any particular function or activity, with the result that statistical analysis becomes impracticable.

THE COMPARATIVE STATEMENT

Since a major purpose of keeping account of income derived from identifiable sources for identifiable expenditure aids in making management decisions, it is important to break down both income and expenditures into functional categories. For example, to record all funds received under a single account titled "Income" would be of little value to the church committee on program planning or to the budget committee.

Let us assume that in Pleasant Hope Church the program planning committee delineated a program that will cost an estimated $75,000. The proposal is submitted to the budget committee, which knows only that total income for the past five years has averaged about $70,000. The records show only total income without a breakdown of receipts into the six to eight separate sources. Such a composite picture makes it difficult for the budget committee to reach an informed opinion as to the potential for increasing specific types or sources of income without the necessity of a great amount of detailed work and analysis. How much easier it would be if there were a comparative year-to-year tabulation of receipts such as the one below.

Pleasant Hope Church
Anywhere, U.S.A.

Comparative Statement of Annual Receipts

Income	1960	1961	1962	1963	1964
Current Offerings	58,964.00	57,845.00	59,125.00	60,460.00	
Arrears Offerings	636.00	480.00	975.00	365.00	
Plate Offerings	1,845.00	1,755.00	1,840.00	1,985.00	
Church School	2,150.00	2,005.00	2,275.00	2,460.00	
Woman's Society	950.00	1,140.00	1,280.00	1,150.00	
Men's Association	1,675.00	1,825.00	1,790.00	1,840.00	
Special Gifts	2,000.00	125.00	660.00	1,285.00	
Miscellaneous Income	64.50	93.25	87.50	102.60	
Total	68,284.50	65,268.25	68,032.50	69,647.60	

Illustration 12. Comparative Statement of Receipts

Which of these sources, if pursued aggressively, may be reasonably expected to produce additional funds? If none, then which proposed departmental programs can be modified with least disadvantage to the major purposes of the total church?

Having determined the sources and the total anticipated income, the church treasurer is concerned with accounting for the authorized expenditure of *all* income and *every* item of payment.

The budget committee has already identified by a "line item" each account in the "Cost and Expense" sections, under the appropriate account title. If it is desirable to establish accounting control over the expenditure of each item of utilities, for example, there should be an account for "Water," another for "Fuel," a third for "Electric Current," and a fourth for "Telephone." If there is no concern for such details, then a single account for "Utilities" will suffice. In the latter case, the periodic reports cannot reveal possible excessive costs in specific items of utilities, with the result that there is no opportunity for curbing extravagance or waste in a particular utility.

Of course, a judgment must be made by some authority on the point of how detailed the accounting shall be—whether any particular item of income or expenditure is to be isolated in a separate account or combined with other related items in an omnibus account such as "Utilities," "Staff Salaries," or "Miscellaneous Income." In making such a decision, it should be borne in mind that period-by-period comparisons for specific items are possible only when such items are accounted for individually, and that accurate budget estimates are based on past records.

Very probably, only a small proportion of churches show churchwide or total receipts and expenditures on the end-of-period financial reports. In some churches, auxiliary organizations—women's societies, men's clubs, youth groups, and church school classes—maintain their separate treasuries and their own records of receipts and expenditures. This situation, or a modification of it, exists even in some churches that "profess" to operate on the "Unified Budget."

THE UNIFIED BUDGET

Good administration does not necessarily dictate that all receipts and expenditures by all groups be handled by the church treasurer, but it does require that "side" operations be included in summary form in terminal financial reports. Some churches achieve this total picture by including each semi-autonomous organization in a section of the "Consolidated Financial Report" at the end of the fiscal year. This practice is strongly recommended on two counts. First, *total accounting* interprets more accurately the *total program* of the church, and, at the same time, gives recognition to the leadership and Christian stewardship of auxiliary organizations. A second valuable concomitant is the opportunities for training that are provided for a number of treasurers and other officers, some of whom will grow into larger spheres of activity and responsibility.

Accounting records will serve their management objectives only when they are properly summarized and issued in meaningful reports to the various officials whose responsibilities relate to them.

All the "operating" departments or committees will depend on monthly or quarterly reports that show current status of expenditures for the period and year-to-date, as compared to previous comparable periods. Such departments as music, education, and publication may be able to modify or expand programs in keeping with budgetary or income limitations. Likewise, the finance committee, by reason of up-to-date financial reporting, will be in better position to encourage a speed-up in collections, or a curtailment of expenditures that can be postponed, if the periodic report shows overdrafts in various departments or in the aggregate.

CASH FLOW CHARTS

Reports for prior and comparable periods will indicate the months of high and low expenditures. On the basis of these reports, cash availability can be planned to meet the peak and valley requirements. The relationship of these data can be shown on a line graph as seen in Illustration 13.

This chart shows that a substantial cash balance carry-over from the previous fiscal period will be needed to meet the excess of expenditures over receipts for January, February, and March. A similar situation exists for August and September. Since a sizable reserve appears on January 1, due to the excess of receipts over expenditures for October, Novem-

CURRENT ANNUAL OPERATING BUDGET $62,600

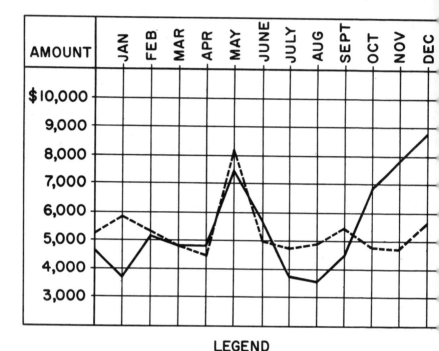

LEGEND

—————— RECEIPTS $64,500

------ EXPENDITURES $62,600

CHART OF CASH NEEDS AND AVAILABILITY
(AVERAGE MONTHLY RECEIPTS AND DISBURSEMENT FOR PAST FIVE YEARS)

Illustration 13. Cash Flow Chart

ber, and December, the deficit for the early months very probably can be met with current income.

The disparity for August and September requires attention. This will require an analysis of large budgetary commitments. Perhaps the anniversary dates for insurance premiums can be shifted, or perhaps outlays for fuel or property maintenance can be postponed to the last three months when receipts are high. The result would be a leveling off of peaks in expenditures to more nearly coincide with the periods of high receipts. The peaks in both receipts and expenditures at May 31 results from meeting accumulated obligations and from efforts of members to pay up overdue pledges. This poses a problem for the financial secretary and suggests a need for regular periodic monthly or quarterly statements of account.

ACCOUNTING TO MEMBERSHIP

Regular and businesslike accounting for stewardship commitments has a salutary effect on the interest and active participation at all levels. This is especially true with respect to reporting to the members on the current status of their personal stewardship. The monthly and quarterly financial report of the treasurer is essential for sound financial management of the total church. It is likewise valuable information for each member as an important part of the total force for good. He deserves also to be regularly informed as to the status of his own participation in the ongoing of the Master's Kingdom. The practice of some churches to "remind" members only when they become delinquent or forgetful at irregular intervals is unsound. Small wonder that poor public relations result and morale sags under such practice. The modern business procedure of sending statements of account regularly is thoroughly consistent with church accounting. Every subscriber to the budget has good reason to expect periodic statements of his contributions. There is no reason to view the receipt of such statements as anything other than an objective business routine for purposes of mutual understanding.

In the absence of labor-saving equipment and procedures, the task of preparing and mailing statements even on a quarterly basis can be time-consuming and an item of large

Second Quarter Ending November 30, 1963

Mr. & Mrs. James Wade
611 Ladies Mile Road
Richmond, Virginia 23227

YOUR RECORD WITH
CENTENARY METHODIST CHURCH

AMOUNT PAID THIS QUARTER			
SUNDAY DATES	UNIFIED BUDGET	SPECIAL	
		PURPOSE	AMOUNT
Sept. 1	4 00		
Sept. 8	4 00		
Sept. 15	4 00		
Sept. 22	4 00		
Sept. 29	4 00	Advocate	3 00
Oct. 6	4 00		
Oct. 13	4 00		
Oct. 20			
Oct. 27			
Nov. 3			
Nov. 10	16 00		
Nov. 17	4 00		
Nov. 24	4 00		
TOTAL	52 00		3 00

YEARLY PLEDGE	208	00
PAID FIRST QUARTER	52	00
PAID SECOND QUARTER	52	00
PAID THIRD QUARTER		
PAID FOURTH QUARTER		
TOTAL PAID TO DATE	104	00
BALANCE ON YEARLY PLEDGE	104	00

ANY DISCREPANCIES SHOULD BE REPORTED TO THE FINANCIAL SECRETARY IMMEDIATELY.

No 975

First Quarter Ending August 31, 1963

Mr. & Mrs. James Wade
611 Ladies Mile Road
Richmond, Virginia 23227

YOUR RECORD WITH
CENTENARY METHODIST CHURCH

AMOUNT PAID THIS QUARTER			
SUNDAY DATES	UNIFIED BUDGET	SPECIAL	
		PURPOSE	AMOUNT
June 2			
June 9			
June 16	12 00	Benv'l.	12 00
June 23	4 00	Organ F.	4 00
June 30	4 00		
July 7	4 00		
July 14			
July 21	8 00		
July 28	4 00		
Aug. 4	4 00		
Aug. 11			
Aug. 18			
Aug. 25	12 00		
TOTAL	52 00		16 00

YEARLY PLEDGE	208	00
PAID FIRST QUARTER	52	00
PAID SECOND QUARTER		
PAID THIRD QUARTER		
PAID FOURTH QUARTER		
TOTAL PAID TO DATE	52	00
BALANCE ON YEARLY PLEDGE	156	00

ANY DISCREPANCIES SHOULD BE REPORTED TO THE FINANCIAL SECRETARY IMMEDIATELY.

Illustration 14. Subscriber's Statement
First and Second Quarters

No   975

No 975		No 975	

Fourth Quarter Ending May 31, 1964 | **Third Quarter Ending February 29, 1964**

Mr. & Mrs. James Wade
611 Ladies Mile Road
Richmond, Virginia 23227

YOUR RECORD WITH
CENTENARY METHODIST CHURCH

Mr. & Mrs. James Wade
611 Ladies Mile Road
Richmond, Virginia 23227

YOUR RECORD WITH
CENTENARY METHODIST CHURCH

AMOUNT PAID THIS QUARTER (Fourth Quarter)

SUNDAY DATES	UNIFIED BUDGET	SPECIAL PURPOSE	AMOUNT
March 1	4 00		
March 8			
March 15			
March 22	10 00		
March 29	10 00	Easter	10 00
April 5	4 00		
April 12			
April 19			
April 26	4 00		
May 3		T.V.	25 00
May 10	10 00		
May 17			
May 24			
May 31	10 00		
TOTAL	52 00		35 00

YEARLY PLEDGE	208 00
PAID FIRST QUARTER	52 00
PAID SECOND QUARTER	52 00
PAID THIRD QUARTER	74 00
PAID FOURTH QUARTER	52 00
TOTAL PAID TO DATE	230 00
BALANCE ON YEARLY PLEDGE	+22 00

ANY DISCREPANCIES SHOULD BE REPORTED TO THE FINANCIAL SECRETARY IMMEDIATELY.

AMOUNT PAID THIS QUARTER (Third Quarter)

SUNDAY DATES	UNIFIED BUDGET	SPECIAL PURPOSE	AMOUNT
Dec. 1			
Dec. 8	10 00		
Dec. 15			
Dec. 22	25 00	Benol.	10 00
Dec. 29	4 00		
Jan. 5	4 00		
Jan. 12			
Jan. 19	8 00		
Jan. 26	4 00		
Feb. 2	4 00		
Feb. 9	10 00		
Feb. 16	5 00		
Feb. 23			
TOTAL	74 00		10 00

YEARLY PLEDGE	208 00
PAID FIRST QUARTER	52 00
PAID SECOND QUARTER	52 00
PAID THIRD QUARTER	74 00
PAID FOURTH QUARTER	
TOTAL PAID TO DATE	178 00
BALANCE ON YEARLY PLEDGE	30 00

ANY DISCREPANCIES SHOULD BE REPORTED TO THE FINANCIAL SECRETARY IMMEDIATELY.

Illustration 15. Subscriber's Statement
Third and Fourth Quarters

expense. Very large churches, because of volume, can well afford machine applications for posting, addressing, and mailing. Smaller churches, for which such machine methods would prove uneconomical, must rely on hand methods that incorporate labor-saving provisions such as one-write systems and window envelopes. Of the several such systems, the one illustrated is applicable to small and large memberships. This variation employs NCR paper that requires no regular carbon paper or spot coating. The original writing is sent in a window envelope to the subscriber at the end of each quarter and the automatic carbon copy is retained in a special binder for a permanent subscriber ledger card.

A variety of printings and arrangements are available to suit the accounting needs of most churches. Another popular style is a quadruplicate spot carbon backed form that cumulates the giving record from the first quarter through the last and provides a ledger card for permanent file as a by-product.

Copy for "Second Quarter" is exposed, filled in, detached, and mailed. The "Third Quarter" and "Fourth Quarter" are completed and mailed in sequence, leaving the composite record for all four quarters on the permanent file record. Next to machine posting, the one-write methods seems most efficient.

Chapter 4

WHO KEEPS THE BOOKS
AND RECORDS OF ACCOUNTS?

What are the minimal qualifications for church accountant?

What are the necessary physical facilities for effective church accounting?

Why is it important to schedule a definite time and place for doing the accounting work?

THE VALUES OF A PLAN

An attempt to conduct the financial affairs of a church without keeping accurate records of its business transactions would be as futile as attempting to sail the seven seas without charts and compass. In both cases, the absence of indicators of movement and direction could be disappointing and even disastrous.

It might be equally true that adequate and well-kept records do not of themselves insure either a safe voyage or a successful operation, but they do help to accomplish the desired objectives.

At least once a year—preferably once a quarter—it is highly desirable to summarize the various sources of receipt and expenditure of funds into reports to be studied and interpreted for future operations. It may be that measures will be necessary to increase the monthly or weekly income or to consider the curtailment of operating expenditures.

Some may argue that the church is not a business and therefore not subject to the same kind of accounting as commercial enterprises. However, the fact remains that there is a temporal base of the church, as well as the spiritual nature, and that certain principles of business finance are applicable. Temporal support of churches and synagogues was a necessity in the early Christian era. Building costs, maintenance of physical property, and salaries had to be paid then as now. Always, budgets must be evolved and subscribed and paid by those for whom the church exists.

Accounting is said to be the "language of business." It is, then, the language of the business side of our church. Individuals who engage in any phase of church management must learn that language.

THE KEEPER OF THE ACCOUNTS

A person who wants to keep the accounts must first be informed on the basic principles and operational procedures of accounting. It is desirable that he understand the principle of equality in the exchange of values in every transaction, as emphasized in Chapter 1. For every increase in one account there is an equal and corresponding increase or decrease in another; a debit for every credit and contrariwise. In order to maintain this equilibrium, absolute accuracy is essential. Therefore, the bookkeeper or accountant must be a *conscientious, careful,* and *meticulous* workman.

Except for very large churches, it is expedient for the church secretary or an office clerk to devote a portion of her time to keeping the church books. In many instances, the job requires only a fractional part of one's time—if an efficient system is used. With a good plan and labor-saving equipment, systematic work procedures and records tailored to the needs of the job, a full-time job may well become a half-time job of the church secretary or an outside worker.

One excellent source of competent labor supply for church accounting may be found in the increasing number of older persons who have expert knowledge of accounting and have retired under Social Security. Persons in this category are able to earn the maximum income, $100 a month, without decreasing Social Security benefits. They may perform a useful service to the church and derive at the same time a large measure of personal satisfaction.

Employment for pay tends to impose on the worker a greater sense of responsibility and encourages greater punctuality than does voluntary employment. It is therefore generally not wise to use part-time employees on a gratis basis. This is desirable, since the requirements in church accounting are competence, consistency, continuity, and responsibility. Free work is inconsistent with sound personnel policy except on an "extracurricular" basis. Even in the church. . . . "the laborer is worthy of his hire" (Luke 10:7).

THE MEDIUM OF ACCOUNTING

Accounting, as one of the major functions of the church office, involves the use of physical properties such as computing machines, books of account, records, business forms of a wide variety, and reports. If "accounting *is* the language of business," the design and use of records come close to being the only medium by which that language is expressed.

The importance of properly designed forms and records in business becomes arresting when we consider that a half dozen multimillion-dollar corporations devote themselves exclusively to designing and supplying specialized records to American business. Gross annual sales of forms by one of these companies alone ran to more than $70,000,000 in 1961.

So crucial is the use of forms that churches of any appreciable size should periodically do a forms-and-records survey of their operations to determine sources of financial losses due to the use of superfluous and poorly designed forms. For churches, it is especially important to study the effectiveness of their forms and records and to analyze needs for more functional paper work.

The basic principle of modern data processing is the "onetime write" procedure. With it, there results not only a saving in recording time but, what is more important, the chances for human error are drastically reduced in posting or transcription of original entry to subsequent records. A more comprehensive study of forms-and-records analyses is contained in the succeeding chapters of this volume as they relate to the various phases of church accounting.

OFFICE SPACE PLANNING

The functionally planned physical office will provide space, equipment, arrangement, and the atmosphere appropriate for accounting work. Extensive or elaborate space may not be needed, but it must be sufficient to accommodate the needs without crowding or stacking machines, appliances, and furniture and without the need to frequently move and adjust them. The allotted space is arranged for convenience and in accordance with the flow of work. For example, the files containing membership records should be located conveniently close to the posting machine or the desk on which posting is done. All sequentially used facilities should be arranged in the order of use.

To determine the best arrangement, professional systems analysts often make cardboard templets of each piece of equipment and furniture to scale. These templets can be moved about on a scale drawing of the room until an acceptable arrangement has been achieved. In old buildings, it sometimes happens that existing doorways, windows, and other fixed architectural features such as heating or cooling registers interfere with the ideal plan. Hence, adjustments and compromises have to be made. If, however, a new building is being planned, or major structural changes are contemplated in the existing building, the accounting office or the accounting space in the business office may be planned so as to make for good arrangements.

The diagram in Illustration 16 suggests an arrangement that is consistent with the sequence of work activities.

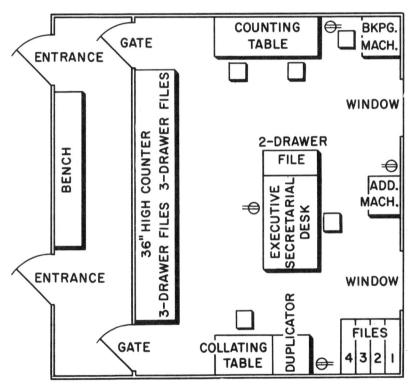

Illustration 16. Business Office Layout

The desk is of the double-pedestal type with typewriter pull-out on the left side and a desk-high working file adjacent to the desk on the right side. An adding machine is located at the rear of the desk, and is readily accessible by swiveling the posture chair. Hence, the two most used machines—typewriter and adding-listing machines—are usable without leaving one's chair. Material in the vertical files is also available within three to four feet of the worker.

To the right side of the office desk is a 72-inch table for counting the offering, assembling papers, and doing similar work. It is kept cleared of all objects on counting days. When used as working space, it will be equipped with two cash trays, money wrappers, memorandum pads, pencils, ink pads, date and deposit stamps, and the other accessories for making up the deposit. This table may be used at other times as a typing table or general work space.

It is suggested that the 36-inch-high counter top house two three-drawer vertical file cases on either side and provide adjustable storage shelving with sliding doors in the center section. Gates with locks from the inside are installed at either end of the counter and a seven-foot bench is included for the comfort of those who wait.

This layout will serve the requirements of a full-time financial secretary or a business manager and as a counting room for the teller committee. While the business office should be reasonably accessible to the public, its arrangement should be such as to insure privacy and security when money is being handled or accounting work is in progress. Therefore, night latches may be desirable for the entrance doors.

Chapter 5

RELATIONSHIP
OF ACCOUNTING
TO BUDGETARY
ADMINISTRATION

To what extent should the schedule of accounts relate to the items in the operating section of the budget? To the nonoperating section?

What are the advantages of making monthly or quarterly status comparisons of year-ago with current budget income, expenditures, and balances?

The budget document is the result of a planned procedure for obtaining and expending funds. It is the written authority for securing and expending such funds. To a great extent, the budget grows out of accounting reports of previous periods and is controlled essentially by the accounting procedures.

HOW MANY ACCOUNTS?

In the operating budget, there is a line item for every account carried in the "Operating Income" and "Operating Expense" section of the ledger. Conversely, there is an account in the ledger for every line item in the operating budget. It is necessary to make a clear distinction here between the "Operating Income and Expenditures" and "Nonoperating Income and Expenditures." The latter classifications are seldom included in the budget document, even as a memorandum, because they do not constitute a direct stewardship responsibility.

If we maintain a unified budget, and if we include in it debt service and property improvement, there remains the transfer account for what sometimes is referred to as "R & D" (Received and Disbursed) or "In & Out" funds. Generally, there is no accurate way of pre-determining these items, and if there were, they would not reflect the central program of the church. However, many of the peripheral activities that constitute "extras," such as subscription to the church paper, contributions to a special offering for disaster relief, and similar events, do reflect Christian motivation and even sacrificial giving, and as such should be reflected in the accounting system. Such items are not shown in the budget because they cannot be known or predicted at the time the budget is made. They may be handled through the church treasury and are properly included in the books of account, but they are recorded in the nonoperating section of the ledger. They are shown also on the nonoperating section of periodic reports.

Another type of R & D recording relates to such items as payment for telephone tolls by outsiders or transfer of values from "operating" bank account to special accounts. For example, a legacy of $1,000 is received for the trustees' fund and is designated as "Organ Fund." It may be received into and paid out of the operating bank account on the same day. It is not an operating receipt and therefore should not be recorded in the "Regular Cash Account" nor shown on the operating statement. This kind of transaction appears only as a memorandum entry and not as a receipt nor as a disbursement in the "Operating Cash Account."

The exception to the statement that all ledger accounts should appear in the budget as line items includes, of course, all fixed assets, liabilities, and all nonoperating income and nonoperating expense items. A comparison of the items and organization of the Budget Document and the Chart of Accounts may readily be seen in the *Budget Work Sheet* shown below. It is an adaptation of the Chart of Accounts.

Spring Hill Church
Anytown, U.S.A.

January 1, 1963

ASSETS: Code 100
- 101   Cash—Regular Account
- 102   Petty Cash
- 103   Stewardship Fund Savings Account
- 104   Church Improvement Fund
         Savings Account
- 105   Benevolence Fund Savings Account
- 106   Trust Funds—Custody of Trustees
- 107   Church Land
- 108   Church Buildings
- 109   Parsonage "A"
- 110   ————————————————
- 111   ————————————————

LIABILITIES: Code 200
         (May be entered in RED on
             Distribution Journal)
- 201   Prepaid Pledges
- 202   Bonds Payable
- 203   Notes Payable
- 204   Accounts Payable
- 205   Accrued Interest Payable
- 206   FICA and Federal Withholding
         Tax Payable
- 207   State Withholding Tax Payable
- 208   Conference Apportionments Payable
- 209   Conference Contributions Payable

	Current Budget	Pro-posed	Increase (+) or De-crease (−)	Adopted
INCOME: Code 300				
301 Current Subscriptions and Contributions	90,000	86,000	2,000	92,000
302 Old Subscriptions	850	850	000	850
303 Plate Offerings	3,600	4,000	400	4,000
304 Registered Attendance	300	350	50	350
305 Initial Offering	190	200	10	200
306 Holy Communion	400	450	00	400
307 Flower Fund	380	400	20	400
308 Special Offerings and Gifts	2,000	2,500	500	2,500
309 Other Income	200	200	00	200
310 R & D Items	00	00	00	00
TOTALS.........	97,920		2,980	100,900

			Current Budget	Proposed	Increase (+) or Decrease (−)	Adopted
COST OF OPERATIONS: Code 400						
410	*Personnel Salaries and Wages*					
	410.1	FICA (Social Security)	1,450	1,508	58	1,508
	410.2	Federal Withholding Tax	00	00	00	00
	410.3	State Withholding	00	00	00	00
	411	Salary of Pastor	9,000	9,500	500	9,500
	411.1	Car Allowance	1,200	1,200	00	1,200
	411.2	Pulpit Supply	100	100	00	100
	412	Salary, Associate Pastor	4,800	5,000	200	5,000
	412.1	Car Allowance	900	1,000	100	1,000
	412.2	Rental Allowance	1,800	1,800	00	1,800
413	Salaries, Music and Choir Costs		4,500	4,800	300	4,800
414	Salaries, Secretary "A" & "B"		7,200	7,500	300	7,500
415	Salary, Hostess		1,200	1,200	00	1,200
416	Salaries and Hourly Rate, Food Service		1,600	1,600	00	1,600
417	Salaries, Sextons "A" & "B" and Maid		10,000	10,300	300	10,300
418	Salaries and Hourly Rate, Nursery		1,800	1,800	00	1,800
419	Salaries and Wages, Other		600	600	00	600
420	*Conference Apportionments*					
	421	World Service	9,100	9,200	00	9,100
	422	Conference Claimants	2,380	2,652	292	2,672
	423	Minimum Salary	925	925	00	925
	424	College Fund	2,750	2,750	00	2,750
	425	Episcopal Fund	280	312	32	312
	426	Golden Cross	100	100	00	100
430	*District Apportionments*					
	431	District Sup't. Salary & Parsonage	450	450	00	450
	432	District Work	935	935	00	935
440	*Church Maintenance Costs*					
	441	Church Property	4,300	6,000	700	5,000
	442	Fuel Costs	3,000	3,000	00	3,000
	443	Utilities (Water and Electric Current)	900	900	00	900
	444	Telephone	300	300	00	300
	445	Printing and Publicity	4,500	4,500	00	4,500
	446	Office Supplies and Equipment	600	600	00	600
	447	Insurance and Fidelity Bond	1,800	2,000	200	2,000
	448	Janitor Supplies	375	400	25	400
	449	Miscellaneous Expense	2,000	1,000	1,000	1,000
450	*Conference Contributions*					
	451	Jurisdictional Ministerial Fund	100	100	00	100
	452	Chaplains Fund	100	100	00	100
	453	One Great Hour of Sharing	100	100	00	100

			Current Budget	Proposed	Increase (+) or Decrease (−)	Adopted
	454	Methodist Student Day	100	100	00	100
	455	Television Ministry	50	50	00	50
	456	Methodist Commission for Overseas Relief	25	25	00	25
460		*Benevolences*				
	461	Richmond Home for Ladies	1,200	1,500	300	1,500
	462	Methodist Childrens' Home	2,000	2,200	200	2,200
	463	Church Extension	2,000	2,000	00	2,000
	464	Missions, Home and Foreign	4,900	4,900	00	4,900
	465	The Hermitage Home for the Aged	800	400	−400	400
	466	Welfare, Local	1,200	1,600	400	1,600
470		*Church Program and Development*				
	471	Food Services	1,600	1,600	00	1,600
	472	Religious Education	2,400	2,600	00	2,400
	473	W S C S	500	500	00	500
	474	Methodist Men	00	00	00	00
	475	Membership and Evangelism	00	473	473	473
	476	————————				
	477	————————				
		Totals..........	$97,920		2,980	100,900

STEPS IN DEVELOPING THE BUDGET

The church budget may be formulated in the following sequential steps.

(1) A conference involving the administrative department heads, or the executive committee, is held several months prior to the date for final adoption of the budget. This body reviews the total program of the church as projected for the ensuing year by the various operating departments The total program is the composite of the several department programs.

(2) The "proposed" program is submitted to the official board or to the congregation for discussion and adoption in revised form.

(3) Copies of the "Budget Work Sheet" similar to the one shown may be distributed to chairmen of all "operating"

committees—groups or organizations that use and contribute funds administered under the budget.

(4) Worksheets are then returned to the budget committee for consideration, revision, and adoption. The privilege of a budget hearing may be provided for those whose requests greatly exceed the previous year's amount and who have indicated good reason for an expanded program.

(5) Final adoption of revised budget and publication and distribution to all members is the last step.

The most difficult problem may be that of securing individual pledges or personal commitments sufficient to cover the proposed program. There are likely to be differences of opinion on the timing of this activity. Some people are by nature cautious and conservative. They will insist on securing the member "pledges" before adopting the budget. Many who have faith and imagination will, on the other hand, first project the program of the church and then seek the implementing funds as a consequence. The demonstrated need becomes the motivating force for the "stewardship commitment." Which approach is correct depends upon your attitude toward your own stewardship responsibility, tempered by your sense of sound financing.

It is highly desirable that all chairmen of operating departments—music, property maintenance, missions, education—and all individual members, receive quarterly reports on the status of their allotments and commitments in order that each group and each member can exercise the concern required to bring his affairs into proper relationship.

Music budgets in many downtown churches will be predominantly for salaries of the director, organist, and a quartet, and, on occasion, for supporting voices. In community churches, there may be much less necessity for "paid artists," and hence more reliance upon voluntary talent. A typical detailed budget prepared by the music committee chairman might be similar to the following one:

MUSIC BUDGET

Spring Hill Church
Anytown, U.S.A.

1. Salaries:

Director and Organist	$4,000.00
Quartet @ $75 Mo. each	3,600.00
Special artists	200.00

2. Choir Costs:

Sheet music	400.00
Dry cleaning and storage	100.00
Miscellaneous costs	100.00
3. Maintenance of Instruments (Property)	600.00
Total Budget	$9,000.00

Although the expenditures from this departmental budget are made by the financial secretary, treasurer, or the church administrator, the responsibility for operating within the approved limits rests with the committee chairmen. The item for maintenance in some churches is included in the property committee budget rather than in music. This account is closely identified with both music and property; hence the variance in budgetary practice. Accounting practice may maintain only two accounts for the music department—salaries and choir costs—if maintenance of instruments is carried by the property committee.

Similar individual and detailed budgets will be prepared by each of the other *operating* departments, commissions, or committee chairmen and operated internally in accordance with the *details* thereof. The details will not be specifically identified in the general budget or in the accounting system, but will be included in larger categories.

Since the details are not identified in the accounting system and hence would not appear in periodic reports to the official body, it devolves upon the committee chairmen to keep his fellow committeemen apprised of the financial status of their operation in detail by occasional written statement.

FORM OF THE PERIODIC REPORT

The format of the periodic report, whether for a single operating department to its members only, or by the church treasurer for the information of the governing body, is useful as a yardstick of progress, and it will be more revealing if shown in relation to previous operating periods.

The practice of showing each item in analogue form for two or more periods as well as its *over* or *under status* provides bases for maximum understanding and utilization. The comparative position and the adjusted rate of spending for the period provides the reasons for speeding up or slowing down of expenditures. A multicolumnar form similar to Illustration 17 tells the story briefly but completely.

This tabulation of receipts and expenditures for February is easily compiled from the ledger accounts and is readily interpreted by almost anyone. However, the treasurer or the finance chairman should offer a brief explanation to insure correct understanding by all.

The amounts in Column 1 are visible reminders of the monthly quotas for both income and expenditures. The amounts in Column 4 relate to the differences for items shown in Columns 3 and 6. In the "Income" section, the preceding minus sign ($-$) indicates failure to collect enough money to match the monthly quota for the elapsed months. The ($-$) amounts therefore represent a shortage or deficit in anticipated receipts. The amounts without the minus sign represent an excess over the anticipated cumulative collections for the particular item.

In the "Expenditures" section of the report, the preceding minus sign ($-$) represents a cumulative overdraft or expenditures in excess of the quota for the elapsed months.

You may observe that the total income through February exceeded the anticipated amounts for January and February

Statement of Operating Income and Expenses for February, 1963

Account Title and Number	Monthly Budget	Actual for February	Year to Date		Progress to Date (+) Excess Balance (−) Short or Overdrawn	Current Account Balances	
			Annual Budget	Total to Date		To Be Collected	To Be Paid Out
	Col. 1	Col. 2	Col. 3	Col. 4	Col. 5	Col. 6	
Income:							
Pledges 301	$5,000.00	$4,850.60	$60,000.00	$11,420.00	$1,420.00	$48,580.00	
Plate 303	200.00	210.30	2,400.00	392.40	− 7.60	2,007.60	
Regular Attendance 304	500.00	420.10	6,000.00	765.30	− 234.70	5,234.70	
Miscellaneous 309	150.00	214.50	1,800.00	325.80	25.80	1,474.20	
Total	$5,850.00	$5,695.50	$70,200.00	$12,903.50*	+$1,203.50	$57,296.50	
Expenditures:							
Staff Salaries 410	$1,000.00	$1,000.00	$12,000.00	$ 2,200.00	$− 200.00		$ 9,800.00
Maintenance 420	300.00	175.00	3,600.00	350.00	250.00		3,250.00
Admin. Expenses 430	700.00	700.00	8,400.00	1,400.00	0.00		7,000.00
Music 440	600.00	550.00	7,200.00	1,350.00	−150.00		5,850.00
Benevolences 460	1,250.00	1,425.25	15,000.00	3,000.00	−500.00		12,000.00
Church Outreach 460	1,500.00	1,523.25	18,000.00	2,850.00	150.00		15,150.00
Christian Ed. 470	400.00	375.00	4,800.00	775.00	25.00		4,025.00
Office Expense 480	50.00	12.50	600.00	42.50	57.50		557.50
Utilities 490	50.00	75.00	600.00	110.25	− 10.25		489.75
Total	$5,850.00	$5,836.25	$70,200.00	$12,077.75**	−$377.75		$58,122.25

Recapitulation: Total Receipts $12,903.50*
Less Total Expenditures −12,077.75**

Excess of Receipts over Expenditures for Feb. $ 825.75
Add Cash Balance Jan. 31   6,182.53

Cash Balance Feb. 28 $ 7,008.28

Illustration 17. Monthly Operating Report

by $1,177.70, although two items fell short of expectations by −7.60 and −234.70 respectively. Likewise, in the "Expenditures" section, there was a total of $377.75 greater expenditures than had been anticipated for the two months, even though three items show overdrafts.

The simple "Recapitulation" statement is desirable to show the relationship between the total receipts and the total payments for the *month of February only*. It shows at a glance the cash position at the end of the particular month. This figure is taken from the cash account in the ledger and must agree with the checkbook stub on this date if all funds have been deposited.

Chapter 6

ACCOUNTING FOR RECEIPTS

What "precautions" should be observed in handling receipts?

What is a good method of handling "R & D" items?

How should receipts for auxiliary groups be handled?

What is a good method of accounting for designated gifts, wills, and legacies?

HANDLING CASH RECEIPTS

One of the most sensitive and perhaps least uniform procedures in church finance is the manner of handling cash receipts. In some instances, church ritual affects the time and method of counting and banking the offering. If the plates with the offering must be returned to the altar for dedication, then counting and proper disposal is necessarily delayed until some time following the close of the services. There are several options in this situation and none are entirely satisfactory: (1) A teller committee may remain after church services for 30 minutes to an hour to count and bank the receipts. (2) The offering is stored until later in the day when a teller committee returns to count and bank. (3) The offering is stored in a safe or night depository until next day when the church staff counts it and makes the bank deposit. Unless there is a necessity for returning the collection to the altar for dedication, it may be taken directly to the counting room and processed during the sermon by a teller committee of appointed laymen. There is an obvious disadvantage to this method, since it deprives the tellers of church attendance. In all of these options, there are disadvantages, inconveniences, and added hazards due to lack of proper security.

On the other hand, it is extremely poor practice to allow even nominal amounts of money to be exposed to the risk of theft or misappropriation overnight or to the accounting of any single individual. It is quite unfair to request any person to assume sole responsibility for handling cash without the protection afforded by a witness and co-signer. Accepted practice dictates that the same person should not be required to handle the cash alone and also to account for envelopes or other supporting memoranda.

A good procedure for handling cash offerings can be established by finding the best answers to these four questions: When? Where? How? Who? Most responsible persons would probably define the "when" by saying, "At the earliest practicable time after the collection." Promptness is the best safeguard against risk of loss through theft, destruction by fire, or misappropriation. A partial solution may be found in placing the contents of the plates in locked pouches and leaving them in the overnight depository of a local bank if one is in reasonable proximity to the church. This compromise, however, may impose a considerable burden on the teller committee on the Monday following, for it necessitates a person or committee going to the bank the next day to make the count and deposit. Only members of the church staff or unemployed laymen can afford to take the time. Generally, banks extend the courtesy of a private room or protected space for such purposes. It is both time-consuming and dangerous to pick the pouch up next day, return it to the church for the count, and take it back for deposit.

If the counting is done at the church, it is highly desirable that a private and secure place be established for continual use—a small room or office that can be closed against all would-be intruders and interruptions. There should be easy access from the sanctuary. It should be equipped with two or more tables or uncluttered desktops, an adding-listing machine, tally sheets, a quick-find index of all members, endorsement stamp with ink pad, money wrappers, deposit tickets, paper clips, rubber bands, pencils, one or more sectional cashier trays, and locked money pouches.

The "how" procedure will be in keeping with the factors and characteristics of the particular circumstances. One method that has been effectively used breaks down to something like this procedure: (Counting is done in the church by a committee of five.)

(1) The committees are set up for one Sunday each month by the chairman of finance and are coordinated alternately by him and the church treasurer, or an appointed team captain.

(2) Specific job duties are established for each member of the teller committee as follows:

COUNTING STATIONS 1 AND 2

MAJOR DUTIES:

Open current envelopes (numbered only) and verify amount of cash with amount written on the envelope.

PROCEDURES:

a. Arrange envelopes in numerical sequence, sorting by 100's, then by 10's, and finally by units.

b. Teller No. 1 opens 100, 300, 500, 700, and 900 series; Teller No. 2 opens 200, 400, 600, 800, 1,000 series and hands opened and verified envelopes to Teller No. 3 (listing machine operator) in proper sequence.

c. Sort coin, currency, and checks to proper tray compartments, turning all currency face-up.

d. When all envelopes have been opened, Tellers No. 1 and

2 count all cash items and record on Counting Slips, initial same, and hand to Teller No. 3 for verification with envelope listing. Recount is made if not in agreement.

e. Combine all cash—current offering, plate, and miscellaneous. Wrap coins, band currency, and put odd-lot coins in envelope for each denomination separately, identifying denomination and total.

f. Turn all cash over to Teller No. 4 with Counting Slips.

COUNTING STATION 3

MAJOR DUTY:

Listing all envelopes on split-keyboard adding machine, showing account number at left and amount at right.

PROCEDURES:

a. Date the audit tape on the machine by using non-add key.

b. List opened and verified current envelopes received from Tellers No. 1 and 2, maintaining numerical sequence. Enter the total on the duplicate Summary Sheet. Compare with actual cash count shown on Counting Slips.

c. List opened and verified miscellaneous envelopes received from Teller No. 4. Total and record on duplicate Summary Sheet. Compare with actual cash count shown on Counting Slip received from Teller No. 4.

d. List Collection Plate Cash from Counting Slip received from Teller No. 5.

e. Give the duplicate of the tapes to Teller No. 5. Put the original tapes and the Summary Report in the box for the office secretary.

COUNTING STATION 4

MAJOR DUTIES:

a. Count Plate Cash.

b. Prepare Deposit Ticket.

PROCEDURES:

a. Separate offering into three portions as it comes from the collectors. (1) current envelopes; (2) miscellaneous envelopes;

(3) plate cash. Hand current envelopes to Stations 1 and 2 and miscellaneous envelopes to Station 5.

b. Count the plate cash. Record the amount on Counting Slips and give to Teller No. 3 after being audited by Teller No. 5.

c. Sort checks by bank numbers and record on Deposit Ticket.

d. Show total checks on Deposit Ticket.

e. Combine all cash—current offering, miscellaneous, and plate. Assist Tellers No. 1 and 2 to wrap coins, band currency, and put odd-lot coins in marked envelopes.

f. Complete Deposit Ticket.

g. Put all cash items and Deposit Ticket in pouch. Lock and deposit in night depository.

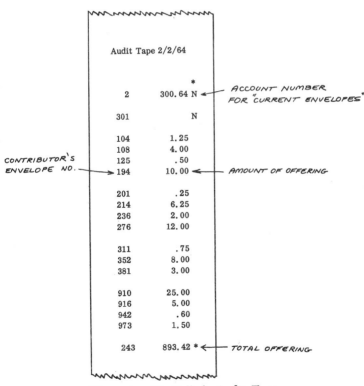

Illustration 18. Teller's Audit Tape

Counting Slip	Counting Slip	Counting Slip

Current Envelopes ΟBL
Offering #301

Plate aCB
Offering #303

Other Income QC
Offering #309

Date 3/3/63 _____
Counters

Date 3/3/63 HR
Counters

Date 3/3/63 KR
Counters

Non-Negotiables:

_____ $ _____

Non-Negotiables:

_____ $ _____

Non-Negotiables:

_____ $ _____

	Envelopes #301	Plate #303	Other Income #309
Total	$ _____	$ _____	$ _____
Total Checks:	$ 574.95	$ —	$ 5.00

Currency:

	#301	#303	#309
$50	$ _____	$ _____	$ —
20	40.00	—	—
10	40.00	10.00	—
5	30.00	—	5.00
2	—	—	—
1	61.00	23.00	1.00
Total	$ 171.00	$ 33.00	$ 6.00

Coin:

	#301	#303	#309
$1	$ —	$ —	$ —
.50	3.00	2.00	—
.25	11.25	3.00	—
.10	2.10	1.70	.20
.05	1.60	.55	—
.01	.20	.10	—
Total	$ 18.15	$ 7.35	$ .20
Grand Total	$ 764.10	$ 40.35	$ 11.20

Counting Slips for use of Tellers 1, 2, 4, and 5

Illustration 18a. Teller's Counting Slips

COUNTING STATION 5

MAJOR DUTIES:

a. Coordinate the work of other tellers.

b. Work miscellaneous envelopes.

PROCEDURES:

    a. Put all envelopes without name in plate cash.

    b. Open remaining envelopes and verify amount by writing in red on the face of the envelopes.

    c. Assign account number to all envelopes that are obviously for pledges by referring to membership book. Transfer these with their contents to Stations 1 and 2.

    d. Record remaining cash on Counting Slip, have it audited by Teller No. 4, and give envelopes and Counting Slips to Teller No. 3 for listing.

    e. Assist Tellers No. 1, 2, and 4 in combining cash, wrapping, and banding for deposit.

(3) On the following banking day, the financial secretary completes the deposit at the bank and makes the appropriate entries in the books of account for all categories of receipts reflected on the Collection Summary Record and receipted deposit ticket.

Member accounts are credited for contributions either from the coded tape or from empty envelopes.

CASH OVER AND SHORT

Cashiers, tellers, and other persons who handle cash and cash items such as checks and drafts find it necessary in some instances to make adjustments for differences between the amount of cash they have on hand and the amount they should have as evidenced by supporting vouchers such as envelope notations. In the procedures outlined above, where several persons (some with little experience in such matters) open envelopes and count the contents, there are likely to be discrepancies between the total listing of amounts on the face of the envelopes and the actual count of the cash.

When discrepancies do occur, there should follow a careful audit of both possible sources of error. Envelopes are checked against the listing machine tape and the cash is recounted by two persons. If more than one type of envelope is used, each type should be listed independently of the

SPRING HILL CHURCH

Anytown, U. S. A.

SUMMARY REPORT OF RECEIPTS

Week of Sunday _____ 196___

Account Numbers	301	302	303	304	305	306	307	308	309	31
Service	Total Offering	Current Envelopes	Last Yr. Envelopes	Loose Plate	Reg'd. Attend.	Initial Offering	Holy Commun.	Flowers	Special Offering	Other Income	R &
9 O'clock	42.11	7.75		16.01	3.00		5.35			10.00	
11 O'clock	1162.44	976.14		62.46		.25		7.50		24.00	
Wednesday	26.96			26.96							
Friday	392.04	336.10				1.00				30.00	24
By Mail	237.00	236.00								1.00	
TOTALS	$1860.55	1555.99		105.43	3.00	1.25	5.35	7.50		65.00	24
Col.	(1)	(2)	(3)	(4)	(5)	(6)	(7)	(8)	(9)	(10)	(11)

Memoranda for numbered columns: Explain unusual entries or circumstances, identifying by column number.

Col. 11 Friday — Older Youth $24.94 Class collection for picni(c)

Col. 10 — $54.00 for Stewardship Fund; $10 for Missions

Col. 10 — Mail — Upper Room subscription

Instructions: Prepare in duplicate for each week.
Original to Financial Secretary.
Duplicate to Church Treasurer.

Teller Committee:

James Corbin

Kenneth Lord

Illustration 19. Weekly Receipts Summary

others. For example, there may be three, four, or more different types of receipts each in its own envelope: (1) Current Offering; (2) Benevolence; (3) Building Fund; (4) Registered Attendance; and (5) Communion.

Finding errors in cash count and in listing numbered envelopes is made much easier if each type of envelope is handled independently until the aggregate balance is verified. Therefore each batch of listed envelopes is kept in sequence as listed until there is agreement between the prepared deposit and the aggregate listing. The deposit and the adding machine tape should also check with the "Total Collection" column of the *Collection Summary Report.*

If the discrepancy persists and shows more cash than envelope listings, it is evident that some account will be credited for an amount less than the actual contribution, or that there was an error in counting the plate offering. If there is less cash than the total face amounts on envelopes, there is a possibility that an account will be credited for too much or that the plate had less than the cash counted. In either instance, the plate account can be used to "force" a balance. Such adjustment should be explained in the memoranda spaces on the *Collection Summary Report* which is signed by two participants.

An alternate manner of handling *Cash Over and Short* is to maintain an account under that title in the ledger. This account may be adjusted with contributors' accounts when errors in them have been established through feedback from the quarterly reports on member contributions. This presumes a debit balance in the *Over* and *Under* account, of course. If a credit balance or *short* condition exists, there is an indication that carelessness exists in the handling or in counting of the cash.

SECURITY MEASURES

Absolute personnel security is seldom achieved in any situation, and perhaps the church has less need for fidelity bonding than any other institution. However, the principle of "safety in numbers," and in continuous vigilance is always appropriate. To repeat what has already been said: no one should ever be placed in a position of handling the envelopes and also accounting for cash without the protection of one or more other responsible persons. No discerning person will allow himself to be exposed to this kind of hazard, and no church or business enterprise need be unprotected against these potential hazards. Theft and fidelity bonds more than justify their nominal cost. Some connectional churches subscribe to fidelity bonds on a broad geographical basis in a group policy. The unit cost is quite small and covers all persons who handle or are in any way exposed to cash.

We have described a system of handling the cash from church collections on Sunday morning in situations where a staff of reasonably accurate workers are available, under conditions of reasonable security. Churches that do not maintain a full-time financial secretary or business manager have the problem of promptly and accurately accounting for receipts that are brought in person or by mail to the office during the week. It is suggested that the system of recording the account number and amount on the split-tape listing machine be carried out for all income at the time of its receipt. If this is done, there will be a machine record from which postings can be made and which will provide a document for audit purposes.

HIDDEN FUNDS

The first of our five Major Premises in the Preface of this volume states that, "If churches are to carry out their mission effectively, their economic affairs must be managed as competently as those of successful commercial businesses." This statement pertains precisely to the accounting function and practice. There is simply no defensible reason for the maintenance of secret funds whose source and amount is known only by a "privy council."

All resources and sources of income from whatever origin should be a matter of record and their uses made in accordance with the judgment of the duly constituted financial authority. The alleged practice of an "inside clique" managing a hidden fund hardly squares with the principles of Christian stewardship, or even with democratic procedures anywhere.

The possible exception to this position is in the case of a "discretionary fund" administered solely and confidentially by the pastor or other authorized persons whose identity may be withheld to protect those who would be embarrassed or otherwise disadvantaged. Although the details of the operation of a discretionary fund should be known only to the pastor or social worker, its existence should be known to the finance officials who will account for it in summary fashion only.

SOURCES OF RECEIPTS

The decision on how detailed to make the sources of income will depend upon what uses you wish to make of income records. Certainly the budget makers will wish to have some detail available, so as to be able to exploit as fully as possible the various potential sources of income. It may be that the volume of certain categories does not justify the effort and expense of isolating and accounting for them. Account Number 302, "Last Year Envelopes," shown on the Weekly Cash Receipts Summary on page 66, may yield such a small amount as to be omitted as a budget item and as a separate account in the ledger.

For the normal operating expenses, the church will look very largely to stewardship commitments of its members. According to statistics from a sampling survey by the National Council of Churches, more than 90 per cent of all church operating costs are borne by the regular tithes and gifts at an average weekly rate of $1.32, or $68.80 per year, for members 13 years of age or older. A typical Protestant church surveyed by the author revealed that 46 per cent of the family units pledged 91 per cent of the annual operating budget for an average family contribution of $4.01 per week. It is evident on the basis of these two unrelated samplings that the bulk of the operating income is realized from the regular gifts of the membership.

For large capital improvements and for plant expansion, most churches must look to legacies, special gifts, and to commercial loans. Capital outlay loans are generally amortized over a relatively long period out of current operating budget, or from special offerings for "Property Improvement" or "Debt Service."

FORMS AND ACCOUNTS

The original source document from which membership accounts are credited is the offering envelope or the accounting tape that is produced from the envelope or personal check.

A wide variety of offering envelopes is available from multiple sources. Some of the styles provide separate pockets for two or more designated funds. Examples of these are Styles "A" and "B" in Illustration 20. The trend of paying by check at the end of the month or longer period makes the multiple pocket envelope inconvenient and consequently little used. Style "C" provides a single pocket but has spaces on the face for allocating the single check to three different purposes. Style "D" presumes contributions for operating expenses only, or leaves it up to the finance officials to make the desired allocation.

Illustration 20. Styles of Offering Envelopes

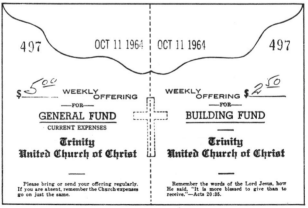

Style "A"

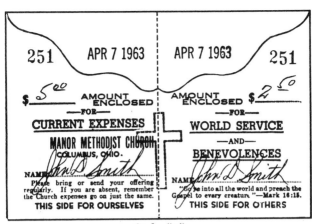

Style "B"

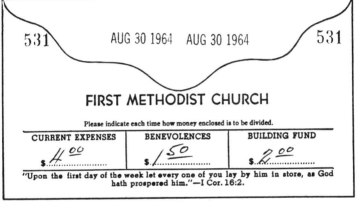

Style "C"

211   OCT 20 1963

My Offering to the Budget of
(The Budget includes Missions, Benevolences, Local Expenses, etc.)

Bethel Presbyterian Church

AMOUNT 7 50

NAME John D. Smith

"Every man according as he purposeth in his heart, so let him give; not grudgingly, or of necessity; for God loveth a cheerful giver."—2 Cor. 9:7.

Style "D"

ACCOUNTING FOR AUXILIARY GROUPS

Even though some churches represent themselves as operating on a "Unified Budget," casual observation makes it obvious that very few actually do. Various and sundry church school classes, youth groups, and special departments often maintain an autonomous treasury and contribute little or nothing to the general operating budget of the church. In most instances, the quarterly and end-of-year reports of the church fail to reflect income and disbursements of these auxiliary groups and hence do not reveal the whole stewardship program of the church.

To achieve a complete portrayal of total church giving, some treasurers have adopted the plan of incorporating the financial records of all active groups in a "Consolidated Report." This is creditable practice, for its provides recognition for achievement of special groups and thereby stimulates further stewardship efforts.

NONOPERATING RECEIPTS

Handling miscellaneous nonoperating receipts and disbursements is a persistent problem. If these items—"R & D" or "Designated Gifts"—are integrated with the regular operating funds on periodic reports, a distorted picture of true operating receipts results. When this happens, there appears to be an over-subscription of the operating budget, while the opposite may be the case.

Good accounting practice dictates that such items previously referred to as "In & Out," "Wash Items," or "R & D" be recorded in the columnar journal under an appropriate heading that provides both debit and credit columns. A brief explanation is sufficient in the journal only. End-of-page or end-of-month posting of the totals *only* to the ledger account is required for control purposes. Totals of the ledger account will appear as an item in the "Nonoperating" section of the periodic report. If there is a debit balance at the close of the fiscal period, it will be shown as a liability and will be a minus value to the cash account if deposited in the regular checking account. An alternate method of handling such items is to maintain a separate "R & D" account with the bank for receiving all such income and from which all appropriate payments are made.

SPECIAL GIFTS, WILLS, AND LEGACIES

If one may judge from financial reports issued by church treasurers, financial secretaries, and finance chairmen, bequests of substantial sums do not ordinarily form a part of the operating structure of the church. With some Protestant denominations, these assets are the exclusive concern of the board of trustees and are accounted for by that body only. These assets often do not appear in the financial reports to the congregation.

Some churches find it desirable to maintain a number of separate funds in savings departments of commercial banks. A principal advantage is the interest that accrues on accumulation of money earmarked for special purposes but not presently needed. The number of separate funds employed will depend upon local circumstances and the accounting system used. Accounting for separate funds may employ the following breakdown:

1. *General Operating Fund.* This is the fund to which all budgeted collections are credited. It is the checking account into which all budgeted receipts are deposited and from which all payments for operating costs are drawn.

2. *Building Fund.* The maintenance of this fund would ordinarily be due to plant expansion, or to contemplated capital outlay needs.

3. *Benevolence Fund.* This fund, like the Building Fund, is carried as a line item in the annual budget and is a well-defined obligation of the stewardship program. Also, similar

to the Building Fund, it may be maintained in a special savings account with interest accumulations.

4. *Restricted Gifts and Memorial Funds.* These funds are generally the responsibility of the trustees. Their administration is legally and ethically determined by the stipulations of the donor, who may direct that the proceeds only may be used for specific purposes. The stipulations may direct the expenditure of the principal in its entirety for an item of furniture, equipment, or other special interests.

5. *Wills and Legacies.* Bequests of this kind are generally restricted as to expenditure of principal or proceeds. To avoid confusion and to comply with the terms of the bequest, it is imperative that these funds not be co-mingled with other funds invested in securities. Therefore, it is necessary that individual capital accounts be maintained for each fund with provisions for continual reflection of earnings, appreciations, and losses in values due to interests, dividends, stock growth, and market decline in securities. After a score or more of years, it may be necessary to ascertain the precise value of any particular gift.

Accounting for special funds implies that separate ledgers accounts be maintained for purposes of compiling the periodic financial statements.

BOOKS OF ACCOUNTS AND ACCOUNT TITLES

Some authority must make a decision as to kind and number of book of original and final entry to be maintained. Following that basic decision, there are details with respect to the title and arrangement of special column and accounts.

Let us assume that we will use a multicolumnar combined "Receipts and Disbursement Journal." Let us assume further that four "Fund Account" controls are carried in the columnar journal and in the ledgers.

This multicolumnar journal is continued on short-cut pages (shown on pp. 84-91) to include the "Income Section," comprising all the sources of recurring receipts, and the "Expense Section," embracing the high-frequency expense accounts. It would not be feasible to provide special columns for all income and expense accounts carried in the ledger. However, provision is made for recording the transactions to ledger accounts by the expedient of the "General Ledger" column, with daily postings to the account named in the "Explanation Column." The "General Ledger" column is in reality a "General Journal" column, since it is used to eliminate the use of a general journal.

THE MANAGEMENT TEAM

If churches "must carry out their business affairs as effectively as commercial businesses," there will be functional organization and specific delegation of duties and responsibilities peculiar to church needs. There must be a clear understanding of each official's role regarding his own relationships to other officials and their responsibilities. Efficient management requires a clearly defined statement of duties and responsibilities for all officials—treasurer, financial secretary, finance chairman, the pastor, and the business administrator.

Although the source of ultimate authority will differ as between congregational and connectional denominations, the basic duties and responsibilities of the local officials are at least similar, if not identical. The need for assigning duties and for pinpointing responsibilities are alike under both types of administration, lest self-appointed leaders, who generally tend to usurp too much authority, assume control. In the absence of clearly assigned areas of operation, the result is likely to be duplication of effort, conflicting decisions, and general confusion of purpose. The "let-George-do-it" type of procedure will not get the job done.

Some *one* person must be assigned to each of the several categories of day-to-day tasks:

I. PLANNING AND REPORTING

    A. Preparing the budget

    B. Planning financial canvass

    C. Presiding over finance committee

    D. Identifying fiscal policies

    E. Reporting to governing body on status of finances

II. FISCAL MANAGEMENT

    A. Negotiate loans

    B. Countersign checks

    C. Make investments

    D. Report to governing body on financial status

III. DIRECTING AND SUPERVISING

    A. Supervise clerical and custodial employees

    B. Authorize purchases

    C. Authorize repairs and maintenance

    D. Coordinate business affairs and operations

    E. Provide insurance protection

    F. Contribute to good public relations

    G. Provide means for quality control for total operation

    H. Provide for outside audit

IV. CLERICAL ACTIVITIES

    A. Counting the receipts

    B. Making the deposit

    C. Recording receipts to individual member records

    D. Preparing periodic reports

    E. Issuing periodic reports or statements to contributors

    F. Keeping complete set of books of account

All these and other identifiable tasks and responsibilities must be performed by someone. The problem: In the absence of a staff business manager, how would you assign each group of duties listed above to one of these: (1) treasurer; (2) chairman of finance committee; (3) financial secretary?

Now, assuming that either a half-time business manager

is employed, assign him to the appropriate category of duties, or to specific duties. It seems abundantly clear that the need is great for a competent coordinator of the many and varied aspects of church business management. The problem may be solved in the employment of a staff church administrator in large churches. The role of the church administrator is seen in a recent statement of the functions of such an official as defined by a large church in Arlington, Virginia. An adaptation of the statement follows.

JOB DESCRIPTION FOR CHURCH ADMINISTRATOR

It has been determined that when a church membership reaches approximately 1,000, or when the budget reaches approximately $100,000, and when the official family recognizes the need for one, an administrator is employed. There is a real value in relieving the pastor of as many administrative duties as possible, so that he can devote more of his time to ministerial and spiritual responsibilities.

Under these circumstances, the church should consider the desirability of a trained layman as church business administrator, to implement the policies and programs of the governing body. The primary functions of the church business administrator are:

(1) *To coordinate all business and fiscal matters of the church.*
   a. Guidance in the preparation of the annual budget
   b. Approval of all disbursements, in accordance with the budget
   c. Supervision in recording of receipts and disbursements
   d. Responsibility for the annual audit
   e. Preparation of financial reports
   f. Maintenance of pledge records
   g. Stewardship cultivation, including undergirding the work of financial campaigns, orientation of new members to the financial policies of the church and solicitation of pledges
   h. Responsibility for proper handling, counting, and depositing of collections and offerings

    i. Consultation and direction concerning memorials and bequests

    j. Maintenance of proper insurance, particularly in the areas of fire and extended coverage, liability, theft, and workmen's compensation

    k. Exercise of proper attention to tax matters

(2) *To manage the physical facilities and temporal affairs of the Church*

    a. Responsibility for the maintenance and appearance of the property

    b. Supervision of the custodial staff

    c. Accomplishment, through the property committee, of needed repairs

    d. Long-range planning of needed facilities and repairs

    e. Negotiation of contracts for services

    f. Purchase of supplies (except educational materials)

    g. Purchase and maintenance of equipment

    h. Supervision of the kitchen and dining facilities in cooperation with the culinary committee

    i. Supervision of the master calendar and assignment of all groups to facilities with the building

(3) *To project the image of the church in its proper relationship to the community as well as to the world.*

    a. Utilization of the facilities of church and news periodicals, church bulletins, local news releases, and radio and television to promote the work and programs of the church

    b. Arrangements for general printing and paid advertising

    c. Responsibility for mailings to the membership, including keeping abreast of postal regulations and maintaining proper accounts with the post office

(4) *To work closely with the personnel committee and to supervise the nonprofessional staff of the church.*

    a. Responsibility for the implementation and coordination of the functions of the secretarial and office personnel

        (a) Provision of opportunity for volunteer workers

        (b) Integration of services of volunteer workers

    b. Assistance to the official board, commissions, and committees in carrying out their policies and procedures, as specifically delegated.

(a) Ex-officio member of the official board
(b) Ex-officio member of the commission on finance
(c) Coordinate the personnel committee

To qualify for this position the person must be a responsible, dedicated Christian layman with a general orientation in the theological concerns of the church, a specific knowledge of the historical background of the denomination, and a working knowledge of the language and organizational structure of the church. He must be a person who can work amicably with all members of the staff, as well as with the entire membership of the church. The individual should be trained and experienced in matters of business administration, but, more important, he must be spiritually committed to this assignment in life.*

* Adapted from Statement of Mount Olivet Methodist Church, Arlington, Va.

Chapter 7

ACCOUNTING FOR DISBURSEMENTS

Why is it important to require signed authorization for all payments?

What is the purpose of maintaining a petty cash fund and how is it used?

How should "nonoperating" receipts and expenditures be handled to avoid confusion in reporting?

All who initiate payments for goods and services have these two important judgments to make for each expenditure:

1. Every payment must have been authorized by a responsible person. The authorization may have been in the form of a stated policy and therefore a continuing one or specific for a single transaction. Generally, the case with respect to making up the regular payroll is a continuing authority. For example, at stated intervals, weekly, semimonthly, or monthly checks are written for stipulated amounts without further direction. When making payment for unscheduled or irregular items, it is necessary that specific

authorization be established by a voucher or some other signed or initialed document. The prudent paymaster will not make expenditures on the basis of oral advice unless he is working under a condition of standing authority for such matters.

2. There arises the problem of charging every expenditure to one or more specified ledger accounts. This procedure emphasizes the necessity of having a standard system of accounts organized into well-defined categories. In order to conform to budgetary provisions and to achieve uniformity in reporting, the same items of expenditure must be consistently charged to the same account. For example, the shade of distinction as between "Office Expense" and "Furniture and Fixtures" when recording the payment for a pencil sharpener and an adding machine must be understood and followed.

A recent review of one church's monthly financial report indicated a charge to "Office Expense" for the secretary's monthly salary. Do you agree with this classification? Still another treasurer would distribute the fuel, water, and electric expense to these three accounts: "Culinary," "Office Expense," and "Church School." In every church, some authority must decide how far to go in breaking down such expense items and whether to prorate them to the several functions or departments that use them.

The degree of breakdown of expenditures into either general or specific categories will depend upon the judgment as to the shades of interpretation to be made in the periodic reports. If it is desirable to reflect the cost of "Electric Current," for example, this item will carry an account itself rather than being consolidated in an account with "Utilities." Unless individual items are distinguished from a broad category, there is no opportunity to exercise budgetary control by comparison with previous period costs.

In a very real sense, the chart of accounts is a blueprint for communicating to the church governing body and finally to the congregation the operation of the church by functions. For example, the make-up of the annual budget for "Benevolences" may be of great interest to the total membership. Or the budget for "Music" may hold considerable interest to members of the finance committee as well as for the congregation. Many specific questions can be asked regarding music. What is the cost of leadership—minister of director? How much is spent for paid voices, or for sheet music, or for guest artists?

ECONOMY OF TIME AND EFFORT

The basic principle of automatic data processing is that a fact or an item of information is written the least possible number of times. The efficient bookkeeper will adopt time- and labor-saving methods of accounting. Every advantage is taken of one-write procedures. Instead of (1) making an original document, (2) recording it in a book or "original entry," (3) posting to a book of permanent entry, and (4) taking off a statement or report, an effort should be made to eliminate as many of these steps as possible. In very large churches, there are greater possibilities for adopting automated processes than exist in those of small and moderate size. In the very small churches, much information can be secured directly from original vouchers, and some facts may even be trusted to memory. In the very large church, modern labor-saving machines and procedures are imperative.

In many instances, various pre-printed forms and streamlined procedures are applicable. An example is the Multicolumnar Cash Journal, which may be organized to consist of three separate sections. The first section is devoted to cash control columns for fund accounting and general journal. The second section comprises the receipts as shown on page 88, and the third section is used for disbursements or operating expenses. A good way to provide a sufficient number of special columns is to short-cut enough sheets so that all frequently recurring income and expenditure accounts are recorded in a control or summary column. Only the total of the columns or the total for the month need be posted to the ledger account. Hence, the possible saving in the posting activity may fall from 35 individual postings a month to 1. The skeleton of such an arrangement is shown in Illustration 21.

PAY BY CHECK

It is almost trite to say that all expenditures should be by check. Only in quite unusual cases will it be necessary to do otherwise. In those rare instances, a signed and dated receipt descriptive of the purpose of payment is required both for evidence of payment and as a source document for accounting purposes. Payment by check affords all parties to the transaction maximum convenience and ultimate protection. The check stub is a valid source from which recording in the Cash Payments Journal of the *payer* is made. The cancelled check becomes a permanent receipt in the files of the payer.

An exception to the rule of "paying by check" arises when payments for sums of nominal amounts must be made momentarily. Payments for small purchases of merchandise or service—for example, an item of office supplies: gummed labels costing 29¢—is made with cash.

In Chapter 2, we discussed and illustrated a type of original entry record that might be kept for the Petty Cash Account. In addition to the three-column journal shown on page 92 (Illustration 22), there will be a permanent account in the ledger to which the totals of the Petty Cash Book will be posted periodically.

	1963	Account Title & Explanation	Acct. Code	Ch. No.	National Bank 100 Deposit	National Bank 100 W/D	Cash Budget 101 Dr.	Cash Budget 101 Cr.
1	June 1	Balance and (Budget)			592 77			
2	2	Interest Earned						
3	3	Deposits for week	300-07	✓	1280 21		1280 21	
4	5	Mrs. A. P. Jarman	807	5448		4 00		4 00
5		Mrs. Lucy Davis	807	5449		50 00		50 00
6		Dominion Home for Aged	801	5450		5 00		5 00
7		C. M. Kyle	402	5451		140 00		140 00
8	7	Deposits – 1st Sunday	300-07	✓	497 51		497 51	
9		John Edwards Salary	404	5452		54 55		54 5.
10		Evelyn Johnson "	404	5453		33 53		33 5.
11		C. B. Lester "	404	5454		46 47		46 4.
12	9	Deposits for Week	300-07	✓	1341 73		1341 73	
13		R. E. Lively, Salary	401	5455		491 83		491 8.
14		R. E. Lively, Travel	411	5456		60 00		60 00
15		C. M. Kyle "	411	5457		60 00		60 00
16		H. B. Karnes "	411	5458		60 00		60 00
17		News Leader	419	5459		11 39		11 3.
18		Ben Franklin Press	418	5460		336 20		336 2.
19	Mc Daniel Envelope Co.	420	5461		154 00		154 0.
20		Hauke Press	418	5462		96 25		96 2.
21		Curles Neck Dairy	425	5463		5 25		5 2.
22		Grant Drug Co.	807	5464		2 20		2 2.
23	16	Deposits for Week	300-07	✓	1622 21		1622 21	
26		R. E. Lively, Salary	401	5470		491 83		491 83
27		C. M. Kyle "	402	5471		416 96		416 9.
28		Joan Black "	403	5472		249 92		249 9.
29		Paula James "	403	5473		249 92		249 9.
30		John Edwards "	404	5474		54 15		54 15
31		Evelyn Johnson "	404	5475		33 53		33 5.
32		C. B. Lester "	404	5476		46 23		46 2.
33	29	Women's Society, Receipts	310	✓	25 00			
34		Women's Society, Payments	310	5477		25 00		
35		Refund Conference Travel HBKC	411	✓	6 00			
36		Ministers Travel – R. E. L.	410	5478		186 20		186 2.
37	30	Totals Forward		✓	6048 95	4464 71	6017 95	4377 7.
38								

Illustration 21. Multicolumnar Cash Journal

84

Asset Accounts

102 Petty Cash		103 Stewards Fund		104 Property Fund		105 Benevolent Fund		106 Special Fund	
Dr.	Cr.	Dr.	Cr.	Dr.	Cr.	Dr.	Cr.	Dr.	Cr.
9 44		187 15		110 25		13 24		2916 24	
		12 06		28 10		104 35			
9 44		1643 25		428 96		1343 19		2916 24	

Illustration 21. (Continued)

Liability Accounts

201 Prepaid Pledges		202 Bonds Payable		203 Notes Payable		204 Accounts Pay.		205 Taxes Payable		206 Interest Pay.	
Dr.	Cr.	Dr.	Cr.	Dr.	Cr.	Dr.	Cr.	Dr.	Cr.	Dr.	Cr.
	2046 00										
									7 07		
									9 16		
									6 64		
									18 44		
								18 44			
								16 80			
								32 94			
								26 16			
								7 07			
								9 16			
								6 64			
								158 32			

Illustration 21. (Continued)

Operating Income Accounts

	207 Gen'l Ledger		300 Pledges New	301 Pledges Old	302 Non-Pledged	303 Plate Offering	304 Reg'd. Attend.	305 Initial Offering	306 Holy Commun.	307 Other Income	308 Altar Flowers	
	Dr.	Cr.	New	Old	Pledged	Offering	Attend.	Offering	Commun.	Income	Dr.	Cr.
			10345 00	1200 00	9000 00	4000 00	400 00	100 00	500 00	100 00		400 00
			906 65	209 80		48 13	14 00	25 36		11 00		
			131 50	338 75		22 01		3 50		1 75		
			1077 10	176 50		72 43	3 50	12 20				
			1335 27	223 00		66 19	6 85			5 00		
	6 00											
	6 00		4088 02	948 05		208 76	24 35	67 96	65 27	17 75		

Illustration 21. (Continued)

309 Special Gifts Dr.	309 Special Gifts Cr.	310 R+D In	310 R+D Out	401 Salaries Pastor	402 Salaries Assoc.	403 Salaries Office	404 Salaries Custod.	405 Salaries Y. Worker	406 Salaries Nursery	407 Music Staff	407 Music Choir
	1600.00			10500.00	4000.00	7500.00	8200.00	450.00	425.00	10340.00	875.0
							54 55				
							53 53				
							46 47				
				491 83							
				491 83							
					416 96						
						241 92					
						241 92					
							54 15				
							33 53				
							46 23				
		25 00									
			25 00								
		25 00	25 00	943 66	416 96	499 84	268 06			443 90	

Illustration 21. (Continued)

Operating Expenses

408 Pulpit Supply	409 Culinary Expense	410 Travel Minister	411 Expense Confrns	412 Rental Allo.	413 FICA taxes	414 Fuel	415 Water	416 Electric	417 Telephone	418 Printing Expense	419 Publicity
100 00	200 00	230 00	300 00	1730 00	900 00	1800 00	200 00	600 00	900 00	2700 00	1800 00
				140 00							
			60 00								
			60 00								
			60 00								
											11 39
										336 20	
										96 25	
		18 00	140 00							432 45	351 29

Illustration 21. (Continued)

89

420 Office Supply	421 Custod'l Supply	422 Prop'ty Maint.	423 Ins. + Fidelity	424 Education Youth	425 Kinderg'n	426 E.M. Canvass	427 Members Evangel.	428 Christn. Soc. Crn.	429 Commn Mission	430 Miscel. Dr.	Expense Cr.
600 00	375 00	6000 00	400 00	1600 00	425 00	300 00	50 00	50 00	50 00		2400 00
154 00											
				5 25							

Illustration 21. (Continued)

90

501 - 507	601 - 607	701 - 703	801 - 808	900		901	
Conference Apportionments	Conference Contributions	District Apportionments	Benevolences Control	Church Improve Dr	Cr.	Project "A"	Pa
(15,510 00)	475 00	(320 00)	(1260 00)			(1900 00)	
			4 00				
			50 00				
			5 00				
			2 20				
			64 20				

Illustration 21. (Continued)

91

When the Petty Cash Fund is established, it is necessary to draw a check for the established limit of the fund and enter it in the Multicolumnar Cash Journal. "Petty Cash" is debited in the "General Ledger" column and cash is automatically credited by entering the amount in the cash payments column and distributing to appropriate special columns. This entry is subsequently posted to the debit side of the Petty Cash Account in the General Ledger and is also entered on the debit side of the Petty Cash Record as shown below:

DATE 1962	ITEMS	Acc't	FOL. Vouch	√	DEBITS	CREDITS	BALANCE
Dec. 1	To Establish	102	96	√	100 00		100 00
6	Culinary help	472	97	√		8 50	91 50
1963							
Jan. 1	Office Expense	446	101	√		1 50	36 50
2	Office Expense	446	102	√		20 00	16 50
4	Misc. Expense	449	103	√		60	15 90
4	Culinary Expense	472	104	√		4 00	11 90
5	To Replenish	102	105	√	88 10		100 00
Jan. 30	Office Expense	446	110	√		7 50	77 50

ACCOUNT NO. 102   SHEET NO. _____
NAME Petty Cash   TERMS
ADDRESS   RATING
CREDIT LIMIT

Illustration 22. Petty Cash Record

The total of the "Paid Out" column of the Petty Cash Record is posted to the Petty Cash Account in the General Ledger periodically, usually at the end of each month. As indicated on page 92, the replenishing check is posted to the Petty Cash Account from the "General Ledger" column of the Multicolumnar Cash Journal daily. As a result of complete posting, the balances of the Petty Cash Account in the ledger and the amount in the "Balance" column of the Petty Cash Record will be identical.

The complete posting from the Petty Cash Record and the Multicolumnar Cash Journal is reflected in all the general ledger accounts affected shown in Illustrations 23a, b, c and d (below and on page 94).

1962 DATE	ITEMS	FOL.	✓	DEBITS	DATE	ITEMS	FOL.	✓	CREDITS	
Dec. 1	To establ.	96		100 00	Dec. 31	Expended	PC1		63 50	
Jan. 5	To replenish	105		88 10	Jan. 31	Expended	PC3		47 10	

Illustration 23a. Account with Petty Cash

1962 DATE	ITEMS	FOL.	✓	DEBITS	DATE	ITEMS	FOL.	✓	CREDITS	
Dec. 6	Petty Cash	97		8 50						
1963 Jan. 4	Petty Cash	104		4 00						

Illustration 23b. Account with Culinary Expense

Illustration 23c. Account with Office Expense

Illustration 23d. Account with Miscellaneous Expense

The person in charge of the Petty Cash Fund is responsible at all times for maintaining accurate records reflecting receipts, payments, and the resulting balance. The petty cash drawer will contain cash and "Paid Out" vouchers totaling the established limit. For example, if the established limit should be $100, as was indicated in the records shown above, the actual cash count plus the sum of vouchers in the drawer will always equal $100.

Usually a policy is established requiring the submission of the vouchers when the cash on hand falls below a certain minimum, say $15. When this minimum has been reached, the cashier will total the vouchers and present them to the treasurer with a requisition for a replenishing check for the total. In the instance cited above, the balance on January 5 had fallen to $11.90. Therefore, vouchers #96 to #104 should total $88.10. The amount of the check required to re-establish the limit of $100.00 will be $88.10.

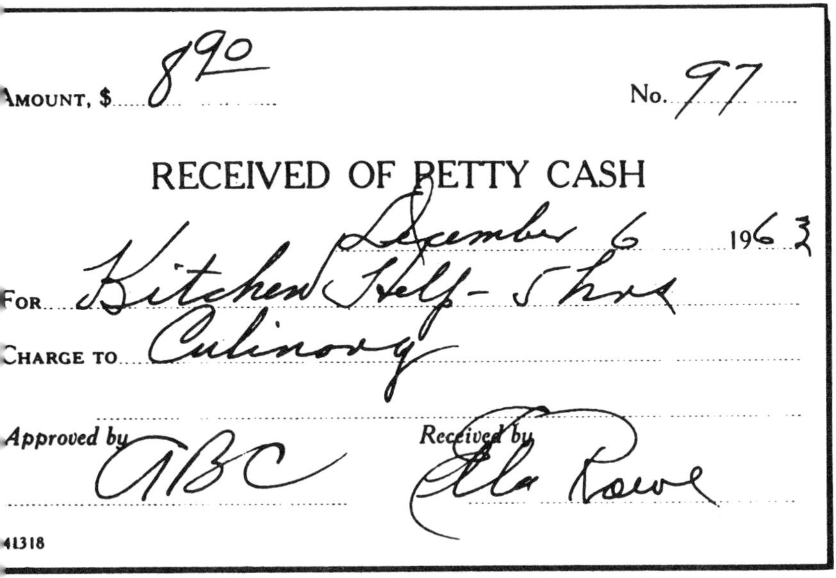

AMOUNT, $ 8 90 No. 97

RECEIVED OF PETTY CASH

December 6 1963

FOR Kitchen Help - 5 hrs

CHARGE TO Culinary

Approved by ABC *Received by* Ella Rowe

41318

Illustration 24. Petty Cash Voucher

The origin of each entry in the Petty Cash Record and eventually in the appropriate Ledger account is the Petty Cash Voucher (see Illustration 24). These vouchers should be kept in serial order as justification for replenishing the Petty Cash Fund and filed for sources of the final audit.

Chapter 8

HOW TO PLAN FOR
CHURCH ACCOUNTING

What kind of account books and appliances are required?

How can specialized machines and devices facilitate the accounting procedures?

What is the advantage of "coding" the chart of accounts?

What basic forms, records, and report blanks are needed?

PURPOSES TO BE SERVED

Designing a system of accounts and the resultant work procedures may be likened to an architect's plans for a house. First, it must be determined what specific needs the various parts will serve. The analogy may be carried further by comparing the chart of accounts with the framework of the building. It is only the structural skeleton of the completed edifice. To the frame will be added many supporting, coordinating, and facilitating accessories. In accounting practice, these will be subsidiary books, supporting records, work procedures, office appliances, and mechanical contrivances.

The complexity of the chart of accounts, the extent of the supporting material, and the pattern of work procedures will depend upon the size of the installation. There is the danger of overorganization as well as failure to plan for enough. Most architects work somewhere between the cottage and the cathedral. The accounting system for churches, too, is somewhere between the large corporation and the corner shoeshop. For our immediate purposes, let us take as an example a church of 1,000 members, having an annual operating budget of $75,000 to $100,000. The full-time staff consists of the pastor, an assistant pastor, the pastor's secretary, one church financial secretary, a part-time minister of music, two custodial workers, a maid, and a business manager.

This church uses a single contribution envelope prenumbered to indicate the member's account. A modified form of the unified budget is in use—the church school, the women's organization, and the men's club and older youth group maintain autonomous budgets. Their financial activities are reflected only as a supplement to the "Consolidated Financial Report" at the end of the fiscal year.

The church owns no property other than the sanctuary and the education building. These assets are financed on a 20-year mortgage, with an annual debt retirement of $6,715.

Before anyone can design a system of accounts and operational procedures with a high degree of accuracy, he must have a clear understanding of what the sources of potential income are, and, in some detail, how it is to be realized. He must know also what the normal expenditures are in terms of the current annual budget. This is to say, the starting point in setting up a system of accounts is the operating budget for receipts and for expenditures. Let us therefore consider the budget shown below as a basis for constructing a system of accounts. Once the system of accounts has been adopted, it will determine the organization of the budget—and not the other way round.

STEP NO. 1. CONSIDER THE BUDGET

You will observe that the "Budget" selected for purposes of stating the problem of designing an accounting system lists only the operating expenditures—a persistent fault of many budget makers. It is quite as important to make a section showing the potential support of operating expenses in terms of receipts. In the absence of an "Income Section," let us assume that the sources of income—and their approximate proportions of the total—will be the following:

Pledged Offerings	80%
Unpledged Offerings	5%
Undesignated Gifts	5%
Plate Offerings	8%
Other Income	2%
Total	100%

A copy of last year's expenditure budget, with groupings arranged for easy understanding by the membership, is indicated below. It is obvious that the grouping of items does not follow a sequence that would serve the accounting needs. Related items of Personnel Costs, Operating Expense, Benevolences, Jurisdictional Apportionments, and Program Development are widely separated in many instances. What we see is a very appropriate statement for public understanding of the church's program under three service catagories—a minister's conception of a public relations release to the membership.

Problem: To design a system of accounts that properly reflect the financial operation of Spring Hill Church in a manner that will make it convenient to prepare financial operating statements at the end of fiscal periods.

Spring Hill Church
Anytown, U.S.A.

OPERATING EXPENSE BUDGET
June 1, 1962–May 31, 1963

OUR MINISTRY TO OTHERS

World Service . . . . $ 9,100.00

Foreign and Home Mission Specials

(Easter Offering)	4,900.00
Committee on Overseas Relief	25.00
Mission Special.	2,000.00
Children's Home (Christmas Offering). . . .	2,000.00
Home for Ladies (Thanksgiving Offering) . .	1,200.00
The Hermitage (Harvest Day Offering) . . .	800.00
Chaplain—Local Institutions.	100.00
One Great Hour of Sharing	100.00
TV Ministry Fund	50.00
Student Day	100.00
Golden Cross	100.00
Welfare	1,200.00
Jurisdictional Ministerial Fund	100.00
Education Fund	2,750.00
District Work	925.00
OUR MINISTRY TO OTHERS—TOTAL	$25,450.00

OUR LOCAL EXPENSES

Ministry of Music	$ 5,000.00
Debt Service	6,715.00
Printing	2,700.00
Publicity	1,800.00
Office Supplies	600.00
Fuel and Utilities	4,250.00
Insurance	1,800.00
Youth Work	1,600.00
Maintenance of Church Property	4,300.00
Culinary Expense.	1,200.00
Pastor's Secretary	3,650.00
Church Secretary	3,650.00
Nursery Workers	425.00
Assistant to the Pastor—Youth Worker . . .	450.00
Sexton	3,250.00
Assistant Sexton	2,620.00
Maid	2,100.00
Janitorial Supplies	375.00
Miscellaneous	3,600.00
OUR LOCAL EXPENSES: TOTAL.	$50,085.00

OUR MINISTERIAL SUPPORT

Pastor's Salary	$10,000.00
Expense—Travel	1,300.00
Associate Pastor's Salary	4,000.00
Expense—Travel	1,000.00
Episcopal Fund	280.00
District Superintendent's Salary and Home .	558.00
Conference Claimants	2,380.00
Minimum Salary Fund	925.00
Associate Pastor's Rental Allowance	1,750.00
Pulpit Supply	100.00
OUR MINISTERIAL SUPPORT: TOTAL	$22,293.00

RECAPITULATION:

OUR MINISTRY TO OTHERS	$25,450.00
OUR LOCAL EXPENSES	$50,085.00
OUR MINISTERIAL SUPPORT	$22,293.00
TOTAL BUDGET FOR CONFERENCE YEAR 1962–63	$97,828.00

STEP NO. 2. DESIGNING ACCOUNTS PATTERN

It is obvious that two primary classifications of any accounting systems do not appear in the budget. In fact, in most financial reports, the two—fixed assets and fixed liabilities—are almost never included except as a separate accounting by the trustees. In most states, trustees are by statute the legally acknowledged corporate owners of church property. Its administration, purchase, and disposal resides in the authority of church-appointed and court-confirmed trustees.

A complete accounting system will nevertheless provide a classified system of accounts to accommodate all four principal types of accounts: *assets,* both current and fixed; *liabilities,* both current and fixed; *income;* and *expenditures.* The fifth class, *net worth,* or *capital,* is not included in church accounting, since the church exists and operates not for financial profit but for the spiritual benefit of man and the glory of God.

Accounts are grouped according to the four types named above and are coded in 100, 200, 300 and 400 order. Several advantages accrue from grouping accounts into functional families and coding for numerical control.

(1) Coding makes strict classification and sub-grouping easy and constant.

(2) In the filing system, which is inevitably interrelated with the accounting plan, it is easy to file and find by code.

(3) It is possible to apply data processing principles and produres to the accounting operation simply by using the *code* for punched cards or tape.

All daily receipts and expenditures can be registered on a split-keyboard adding machine using code number for account designation, the amount in add position for receipts and in subtract position for payments.

There is never a pat way of setting up a system. Each set of circumstances make necessary adjustments and innovations to suit the particular need. Examine the chart of accounts that follows in the light of the budget information that is shown on pages 101-104. To what extent does the system of accounts meet the needs expressed in the budget? To what extent is there incompatibility?

Spring Hill Church
Anytown, U.S.A.

CHART OF ACCOUNTS

ASSETS: 100 Class

101 Current Cash Operations
102 Petty Cash
103 Stewardship Savings Account
104 Church Improvement Savings Account

105 Benevolence Fund Savings Account
106 Church Trust Funds (Trustees' Accounts)
107 Church Land
108 Church Buildings
109 Parsonage "A"

LIABILITY ACCOUNTS: 200 Class

201 Prepaid Pledges
202 Bonds Payable
203 Notes Payable
204 Accounts Payable
205 Accrued Interest Payable
206 FICA and Federal Withholding Taxes Payable
207 State Withholding Taxes Payable
208 Conference Apportionments Payable
209 Conference Contributions Payable

INCOME: 300 Class

301 Current Subscriptions and Gifts
302 Old Subscriptions
303 Plate Offerings
304 Registered Attendance
305 Initial Offerings
306 Holy Communion
307 Flower Fund
308 Special Offerings and Gifts
309 Other Income
310 Received and Disbursed (Nonoperation)

COST OF OPERATIONS: 400 Class

410 *Personnel Salaries and Wages* (Total Only)
  410.1 FICA (Social Security)
411 Salary of Pastor
  411.1 Car Allowance
  411.2 Pulpit Supply
412 Salary of Associate Pastor
  412.1 Car Allowance

412.2 Rental Allowance (Parsonage "B")
413 Salaries, Music, and Choir Costs
414 Salaries, Secretaries "A" & "B"
415 Salary, Hostess
416 Salaries and Hourly Rate, Food Service
417 Salaries, Sextons "A" & "B," and Maid
418 Salaries and Hourly Rate, Nursery
419 Salaries and Wages, Other

420 *Conference Apportionments* (Total Only)
421 World Service
422 Conference Claimants
423 Minimum Salary Fund
424 College Fund
425 Episcopal Fund
426 Golden Cross

430 *District Apportionments* (Total Only)
431 District Superintendent's Salary & Parsonage
432 District Work

440 *Church Maintenance Costs* (Total Only)
441 Church Property
442 Fuel Costs
443 Utilities (Water & Electricity)
444 Telephone
445 Printing and Publicity
446 Office Supplies and Equipment
447 Insurance and Fidelity Bonds
448 Custodial Supplies
449 Miscellaneous Expenses

450 *Conference Contributions* (Total Only)
451 Jurisdictional Ministerial Fund
452 Chaplain's Fund
453 One Great Hour of Sharing
454 Methodist Student Day
455 Television Ministry
456 Methodist Commission for Overseas Relief

460 *Benevolences* (Total Only)
  461 Richmond Home for Ladies
  462 Methodist Childrens Home
  463 Church Extension
  464 Missions, Home and Foreign
  465 The Hermitage Home for the Aged
  466 Welfare, Local

470 *Church Program and Development* (Total Only)
  471 Food Services
  472 Religious Education
  473 WSCS
  474 Methodist Men
  475 Membership and Evangelism

STEP NO. 3. BUILDING THE SYSTEM

The accounting plan may be ever so well tailored so that it encompasses all the budget items and supplies details for the periodic reports, yet fails to function because of lack of proper procedures, adequate equipment, appliances, and forms.

A space well arranged, and equipped with desks, files, machine, and appliances necessary for the accounting tasks was emphasized in Chapter 4. You may wish to turn back to the chart on page 47 and review the layout in connection with the present consideration of a well-appointed space with reasonable privacy, security, and accessibility to related offices and activities.

BOOKS OF RECORD

The General Ledger is the source of summarized information from which to draw in the preparation of periodic reports, for answering inquiries about existing balances, establishing current values of property, and reviewing facts pertaining to previous periods of operations. For all these purposes, it is recommended that a loose-leaf book be kept with vertical money columns for "Debits," "Credits," and

"Balance." With this arrangement, it is easy to shift position of sheets for correct sequence of coded accounts. This form also enables the bookkeeper to keep the current balances of all accounts up to date without the necessity of ruling and balancing at the close of the fiscal period. It is necessary only to underscore the end-of-year balance in red in order to make it stand out for quick reference.

At the beginning of each year, the amounts budgeted to income accounts are entered in the *debit* column in red or green. Daily, or at the end of each month, total receipts are posted from the book of original entry (Multicolumnar Cash Journal) to the credit column and the resulting balances are extended in red or green. The balance of such income accounts as "Current Subscriptions" represents the remaining amount to be raised to meet the budget estimate. If the budget is equaled, the balance will be entered in black and will represent an excess over amount budgeted. (See Illustration 25, page 106.)

Expenditure accounts are credited in *black* for the approved budget amount at the beginning of the fiscal year to represent the amount due the account from the total budget. As expenditures are made, the account is debited as totals of special columns in the Multicolumnar Cash Journal or from the "General Ledger" column entries. Balances are forwarded in *black* until the account is overdrawn, in which case the credit balance is shown in red. (See Illustration 26—Office Supplies and Equipment—on page 106.)

The Subscriptions Ledger takes a variety of forms, as was explained in a previous chapter. Some financial secretaries maintain a bound book in essentially the same form as the general ledger, which is illustrated above, with a sheet allotted to each subscriber. Other church accountants maintain a visible file of specially printed cards for recording amount pledged, dates and amounts of payments, and a space for special gifts. In keeping with the aforementioned

ACCOUNT NO. 301					SHEET NO. _____	
NAME Current Subscriptions			TERMS			
ADDRESS			RATING			
			CREDIT LIMIT			

DATE 1963	ITEMS	FOL.	✓	DEBITS	CREDITS	BALANCE
June 1	Budget adopted 5-15-63			100000 00		100000 00
30	Collections for June	G 1			9246 20	90753 80
July 30	Collections for month	G 2			8619 80	82134 00
Aug. 31	" " "	G 4			6715 24	75418 76
Sept. 30	" " "	G 5			8826 18	66592 58
Oct. 31	" " "	G 7			9075 71	57516 87
Nov. 30	" " "	G 8			8934 16	48582 71
Dec. 31	" " "	G 9			7794 47	40788 24
1964 Jan. 31	" " "	G 10			4682 90	36105 34
Feb. 29	" " "	G 11			6112 10	29993 24
Mar. 31	" " "	G 12			5418 15	24575 09
Apr. 30	" " "	G 14			7002 60	2422 51
May 31	" " "	G 15			6814 20	9241 71

Illustration 25. Current Subscription Control Account

Illustration 26. Office Supplies Control Account

ACCOUNT NO. 446					SHEET NO. _____	
NAME Office Supplies & Equipment			TERMS			
ADDRESS			RATING			
			CREDIT LIMIT			

DATE 1963	ITEMS	FOL.	✓	DEBITS	CREDITS	BALANCE
June 1	Approved Budget	✓			600 —	600 —
30	Monthly Expenditures	Cv 1		64 18		535 82
July 31	" "	Cv 2		34 60		501 22
Aug. 31	" "	Cv 4		184 30		316 92
Sept. 30	" "	Cv 5		21 80		295 12
Nov. 30	" "	Cv 6		83 19		211 93
Dec. 31	" "	Cv 8		44 61		167 32
1964 Feb. 28	" "	Cv 11		18 36		148 96
Mar. 31	" "	Cv 12		61 15		87 81
Apr. 30	" "	Cv 14		56 20		31 61
May 31	" "	Cv 15		76 32		(44 71)

one-write method, time- and labor-conscious administrators use carbon snap-out quintuplet forms with spaces for regular offerings for each week of successive quarters, spaces for special offerings, and summary of givings to date. At the end of the first quarter, the second copy is detached, placed in a window envelope, and mailed to each subscriber. The form is pre-addressed in five copies. The first copy is an original of each quarter and is retained in the office files as permanent record. An optional one-write system uses a spot carbon or an NCR paper record as described in Chapter 3.

There are many variations of the record-statement form for the Subscriptions Ledger. Some are applicable to hand posting, others are intended for machine posting. The two styles shown below will illustrate a one-write system that

Illustration 27. Inventory and Depreciation Card

EQUIPMENT INVENTORY   Item No. *101*

Item *Typewriter* Date Acquired *6/30/60* Serial *E-987542* Model *250*

	Maintenance Expense Record			Depreciation Record			
Date	Description	Charges		Beginning Value	Jan. 1	Less Deprec.	Present Value	Dec. 31
12/20/61	adjust	$ N.C.		$ 250.00	19 60	50.00	$ 220.00	19 60
5/5/62	Repairs	4	50	200.00	19 61	50.00	150.00	19 61
7/1/62	Cleaned	7	50	150.00	19 62	50.00	100.00	19 62
					19___			19___
					19___			19___
					19___			19___
					19___			19___
					19___			19___
					19___			19___

produces a quarterly statement for the contributor ready for mailing in a window envelope and an original ledger sheet for machine posting with a simultaneous statement. Many similar forms provide for simultaneous preparation of monthly or quarterly statements.

The Petty Cash Record previously discussed and illustrated, and the checkbook with voucher stub, comprise the fourth and fifth primary documents of the accounting system. It is these books—Multicolumnar Cash Journal; General Ledger; Subscriptions Ledger; Petty Cash Book; and the Checkbook—that will be subject to regular audit.

There are also auxiliary and supporting records, such as the *item cards* for each piece of office, kitchen, custodial and musical equipment. These are used for keeping account of original cost, date of acquisition, maintenance expense and depreciation expense, and furnish source data for accounting.

CHURCH MANAGEMENT PERSONNEL

In too many churches operating without business managers or full-time financial secretaries, there is a very great lag between what needs to be done in streamlining work procedures and what is actually accomplished. The old adage, "What's everyone's business is no one's business," holds quite true here. A layman, even though he be highly competent, often does an inadequate job of handling church business management when under heavy stress of his regular job. It is often a hit-or-miss situation unless a strict schedule is maintained for his "church work."

MACHINES AND APPLIANCES

The number, kind, and use of labor-saving office equipment will depend very largely on the volume of data to be handled and the attitude of those in authority. If management is not efficiency minded—just willing to maintain the status quo regardless of the cost in terms of man hours—it is unlikely that much will be accomplished in up-dating office procedures. Also, if the attitude and abilities of the financial secretary are inflexible, there is not much opportunity for adopting new routines, regardless of their merit.

For churches having as many as 1,000 members and an operating budget of $75,000 or more, the following labor-saving equipment and appliances are appropriate:

1. *Computing Machine:*
    a. Minimum: An 8-column electric adding machine with credit balance.
    b. Desirable: A 10-column, split keyboard adding machine and a small posting machine with movable carriage.

2. *Addressing Equipment:*
    a. Minimum: (1) Multiple-Part Set of gummed addressing labels (normally 2-, 3-, 4-, 5-, or 6-Part Sets); or (2) Spirit Duplicating appliance, such as, Zip-O-Riter or Handi-Addresser.
    b. Desirable: Metal or plastic embossed plate or typed stencil machine, hand operated (Addressograph or equal).

3. *Filing Equipment:*
    a. Minimum: (1) One or more vertical file cabinets with alphabetic guides and folders.
       (2) Card file trays for 3″ x 5″, 4″ x 6″ and 6″ x 8″ with alphabetic, geographic, and/or numeric guides.
       (3) Rolldex or similar "quick find" name file and account number relative index with geographical code.

4. *Duplicating Equipment:*
    a. Minimum:
       (1) Cellulose stencil ink duplicator with styli, lettering guides, and screens.
       (2) Spirit duplicator.
       (3) Office photo copying device.

5. *Miscellaneous Appliances:*
    a. Minimum:
        (1) Automatic numbering machine.
        (2) Paper trimmer—18 inch.
        (3) Paper punch.
        (4) Stapler.
        (5) Alphabetic–Numeric Sorter.
        (6) Pencil sharpeners.
        (7) Date and time stamp.
        (8) Postal scales.
        (9) Payroll tax computer.
6. *Storage cabinets to suit needs.*

These office accessories will be immensely helpful in keep
ing the church business office organized and capable o
carrying out the accounting function.

Chapter 9

END-OF-YEAR REPORTING

How are balances of accounts determined quickly and accurately?

What kind of information should be shown on:
(1) Weekly Reports (2) Monthly Reports?
(3) Quarterly Reports? (4) Annual Reports?

For whom should reports be provided?

How can periodic reports aid in church management?

The primary purpose of keeping accounts for any church is to enable management officials and constituent members to know precisely the results of the various operations on a given date and over a given period. Unless it is possible to determine quickly and with positive assurance what the status is of all segments of operations, the system is not meeting the need for current control nor for future operations.

With a single-entry method of record keeping, it is sometimes difficult and time-consuming to determine the current status of a particular source of income or item of expense. We learned earlier in this handbook that finding the total additions to and deductions from any given fund required a detailed inspection of all entries and the tedious listing of each category separately. Let us assume that the accounts are maintained on a well-designed double entry system such as we described in the previous chapter. If the Multicolumnar Cash Journal is faithfully and accurately kept and is posted to the General Ledger as planned, finding the balances of all accounts is quick and easy. For accounts having special or control columns in the Multicolumnar Journal, such as *cash,* not only are the current balances available but the contributing detail can be readily seen also.

THE WEEKLY SUMMARY STATEMENT

In all well-run church accounting systems there are checkpoints calculated to show progress and assist in establishing trends in items of income and expenditures. These can be set over against estimates of planned operations—the annual budget. The lapse of time between these checkpoints is determined by those in authority and in relation to the nature of the activity.

Cash, being the most sensitive of all accounts, is of continuing concern. It is fairly common practice for commercial business and the government to establish the cash balance at the end of each day. Most churches find it advisable to require a statement of the cash position at the end of each week. This is the subject of a formal typed report to the treasurer and finance chairman every Saturday for the current week ending. The following form, or something similar to it, may be used. Whatever form is adopted should be used consistently for comparative purposes. The statement should reflect the cash balances of all special fund accounts and the regular operating cash account.

END-OF-MONTH REPORTING

Whereas the weekly report which emphasizes the "Cash Position," is of primary interest only to the treasurer and chairman of finance, End-of-Month Reports are of concern to a much larger group and embrace an expanded type of accounting and management information.

SPRING HILL CHURCH

Anytown, U. S. A.

STATEMENT OF CASH POSITION

Week Ending 3/2 19 63

A. Summary on Deposits, Disbursements, and Account Balances

Date	Description	OPERATING Checking Account	FUND ACCOUNTS Church Improvement	Benevolent Fund	Stewardship Emphasis
	Beginning Balances:	2,717.08	677.15	8,013.24	2,110.25
	Add Deposits: (B)	1,309.84	443 00	———	———
	TOTALS	4,026.92	1,120.15		
	Deduct Disbursements: (C)	1,799.09			
	Ending Balances:	2,227.83	1,120.15	8,013.24	2,110.25

B. Detail on Deposits

Date	Source	Amount
2/25	4th Sun.	1,021.89
2/27	Wed.	178.41
2/28	Mail	31.54
2/28	Mail	78.00

Total Deposits $1,309.84

D. Remarks:
$443.00 received from interest on savings account

C. Detail on Disbursements

Date	Description–Payee	Check No.	Account No.	Amount
2/26	Telephone Co.	5231	444	80.51
2/26	Todd Florist	5232	449	38.20
2/28	Central Plants	5233	441	171.75
2/28	Helms Dairy	5234	472	4.20
2/28	Cg. Supply Co.	5235	448	12.15
2/28	Frank Wendt	5236	411	115.50
2/28	Multigraph	5237	446	10.32
2/28	Acme Print.	5238	445	255.40
2/28	Car Allow.	5239	410.11	95.66
2/28	Staff Salary	5240	410	1,015.40

Total Disbursements $1,799.09

Illustration 28. Weekly Statement Cash Position

113

Here is another checkpoint in the budgetary progress of the church. At each of these twelve monthly checkpoints, it is necessary to assess the progress toward goals that were set in the budget document. It is desirable at these points to compare the current month's income, expenditures, and cash balance with the same month a year ago and to show cumulative year-to-date amounts. Your attention is again directed to Illustration 6 in Chapter 1 for a suggestion as to the form the End-of-Month Report may take.

This is essentially a summary report on the status of every budgeted item. Total monthly expenditures are compared with the monthly allocation. The cumulative expenditure is seen in relation to its cumulative allotment in terms of the unspent (under) funds or the amount of overdraft indicated by the preceding minus (−) sign. The difference between Column 1 ("Annual Budget") and Column 4 ("Spent to Date") shows for *each budgeted item* the current balance of unspent funds or the overdraft. Item totals and balances must agree with the General Ledger account *balances* for this date.

In addition to this expenditure analysis of the budget, it is necessary also to provide a progress report on the income —a phase of periodic reporting that is often omitted in reporting to church officials on the status of church finances. It should never be assumed that income is entirely automatic simply because subscriptions have been secured. An accurate assessment of the flow of income is quite as important as a knowledge of the level of expenditures. One feeds on the other. Therefore, it would seem equally important to employ appropriate means to stimulate income as it is to curtail expenditures when the cash account reaches a critical point.

The End-of-Month or End-of-Quarter reports to the official body should, therefore, provide summary information on both Operating Income and Operating Expenditures in

SPRING HILL CHURCH

Anytown, U. S. A.

FINANCIAL STATEMENT OF OPERATIONS FOR THE

MONTH OF _Aug._ 19 _63_

OPERATING INCOME:	Total Annual Budget	Monthly Budget	Amount this Month	Received to Date	Over, or –Under Budget Est.	Balance Anticipated
301 Current Stewardship	96,000	8,000	7,800	22,400	– 1,600	73,600
302 Uncommitted Income						
303 Plate Offerings						
304 Registered Attend.						
305 Initial Offering						
306 Holy Communion						
307 Chancel Flowers						
308 Special Gifts						
309 Other Income						
Totals						

OPERATING EXPENDITURES:	Total Annual Budget	Monthly Budget	Spent this Month	Spent to Date	Over, or –Under Budget Est.	Current Balance
410 Personnel:						
411.1 Pastor's Salary	9,600	800	800	2400	—	7,200
411.1 Car Allow.	1,200	100	96	320	–20	880
411.2 Pulpit Supply						
412 Asst. Pastor Sal.						
412.1 Car Allow.						
412.2 Rent Allow.						
413 Secretarial Salaries						
414 Hostess Salary						
415 Culinary Salary and Hourly Wages						
416 Nursery Salaries and Hourly Wages						
417 Janitor Sal. & Wages						

Illustration 29. Statement of Budget Position

Illustration 29. (Continued)

OPERATING EXPENDITURES:	Total Annual Budget	Monthly Budget	Spent this Month	Spent to Date	Over, or –Under Budget Est.	Current Balance
418 FICA & Fed. Withholding	——	——	——	——	——	——
419 State Withholding	——	——	——	——	——	——
420 Conference Apportionments						
421 World Service	——	——	——	——	——	——
422 Conference Claimants	——	——	——	——	——	——
423 Minimum Salary	——	——	——	——	——	——
424 College Fund	——	——	——	——	——	——
425 Episcopal Fund	——	——	——	——	——	——
426 Golden Cross	——	——	——	——	——	——
430 District Apportionments						
431 Dist. Supt. Salary and Parsonage	——	——	——	——	——	——
432 District Work	——	——	——	——	——	——
440 Church Maintenance:						
441 Property	——	——	——	——	——	——
442 Fuel	——	——	——	——	——	——
443 Utilities	——	——	——	——	——	——
444 Telephone	——	——	——	——	——	——
445 Printing and Pub.	——	——	——	——	——	——
446 Office Supplies & Equipment	——	——	——	——	——	——
447 Insurance and Fidelity Bond	——	——	——	——	——	——
448 Janitor Supplies	——	——	——	——	——	——
449 Miscellaneous Exp.	——	——	——	——	——	——
450 Conference Contributions:						
451 Juris. Ministerial Fund	——	——	——	——	——	——
452 Chaplain's Fund	——	——	——	——	——	——
453 One Great Hour of Sharing	——	——	——	——	——	——
454 Methodist Student Day	——	——	——	——	——	——
455 Television Ministry						
456 MCOR						

Illustration 29. (Continued)

OPERATING EXPENDITURES:	Total Annual Budget	Monthly Budget	Spent this Month	Spent to Date	Over, or –Under Budget Est.	Current Balance
460 Benevolences:						
461 Richmond Home for Ladies	___	___	___	___	___	___
462 Methodist Children's Home	___	___	___	___	___	___
463 Church Expansion	___	___	___	___	___	___
464 Missions -- Home and Foreign	___	___	___	___	___	___
465 The Hermitage Home for the Aged	___	___	___	___	___	___
466 Welfare	___	___	___	___	___	___
470 Church Program and Development:						
471 Food Services	___	___	___	___	___	___
472 Religious Education	___	___	___	___	___	___
473 Woman's Society of Christian Service	___	___	___	___	___	___
474 Methodist Men	___	___	___	___	___	___
475 Membership and Evangelism	___	___	___	___	___	___
476 _____						
477 _____						
478 _____						

RECAPITULATION:

Total Budgeted Operating Income $ _____

Pro rata to date ----------------- _____

Received to date ---------------- _____

Oversubscribed or Deficit _____ _____
(Show Deficit in red)

Total Budgeted Operating Expend. $ _____

Pro rata to date -------------- _____

Expended to date ------------- _____

Reserve or Overdrawn to date ---- _____
(Show Overdrawn in red)

Current Cash Operating Fund Balance $ _____

relation to budget estimates. The following format is suggested as one way of compiling a comprehensive financial report to members of the finance commission and the official board or other governing body of the church.

REPORTING TO TOTAL MEMBERSHIP

Reference has already been made to the desirability of reporting regularly to the congregation concerning their individual stewardship commitments. An informed constituency is generally a more active body than one that does not receive timely and accurate information. Therefore, it is deemed both wise and expedient to supply the total membership with information on the financial status and needs of their church. A very simple and convenient procedure is to carry a boxed announcement in the bulletin—an analysis with or without explanatory notes such as the following:

Annual Operating Budget	$96,000.00
Amount to be raised for 5 months	40,000.00
Amount received for 5 months	38,245.60
Amount short of goal to date	$ 1,754.40

This simple announcement implies that those who are in arrears with their stewardship commitments should bring their account up to date. This type of reminder to the total membership, in bold type and attractively captioned, can be very effective when used three or four times a year. A more direct approach, and one that can be accomplished in an unoffensive and genuinely businesslike manner, is to enclose a copy of the End-of-Month Report previously described and illustrated with the quarterly statement of account.

END-OF-YEAR REPORTING

The form of terminal, or end-of-year reports, need not differ essentially from the monthly report discussed above, except that it should be somewhat more comprehensive.

Chapter 10

THE PERIODIC AUDIT

What are the purposes of an audit?

By what authority is the audit made, and who makes it?

What is the scope of the "complete" audit?

How can the audit be used as an instrument of planning?

The basis for the audit is not necessarily suspicion of incompetence of malfeasance. It should, therefore, not be looked upon as an indication of distrust or lack of confidence. On the contrary, an audit, whether financial or operational, is all objective and impersonal evaluation of the church's various procedures and functions relating to finances and programmed activities. Among its primary purposes are the discovery of errors in judgment and organization. A complete audit should result in the detection of errors, whether intentional or through carelessness. A constructive audit will indicate ways of improving future operations in terms of fiscal procedures and efficient uses of personnel resources.

THE INTERNAL AUDIT

The internal or self-audit is not only periodic but should be a continuous process of examination and evaluation of over-all performance. It will insure that financial accounting and reporting accurately portray the hard facts in the case. The processes of the continuous internal audit can be a very effective means of maintaining open lines of communication between the church administrator and all other staff members who have interrelated interests.

By detecting deviations from established policy, the auditor can contribute significantly to the improvement of operations of all departments. The self-audit has been aptly described as "a periodic inventory of the management of an enterprise by its own managers. It includes an appraisal of where the enterprise has been, where it is now, and where it will probably be at some future specific time." In this frame of reference, the church is not unlike the commercial enterprise.

If we were correct in our previous definition of the budget as "a planned program of activities and achievements," it is highly appropriate that a critical and objective appraisal be made at certain intervals to determine to what extent the accomplishments match the projections. Not only are checks made on the accuracy of the accounting records, but there is a review of projects, activities, organization, and procedures. There is a comparison between what was expected to be accomplished and what actually was achieved. Not only are deviations observed, but faithful compliance as well. From this base, remedial measures can be undertaken.

THE EXTERNAL AUDIT

In addition to the self-audit, the church officials should provide for an outside audit by competent and responsible authority. Many churches are truly "big business" in terms of finances alone. But even the handling of nominal sums of cash suggests the desirability, if not the necessity, for a financial audit by certified public accountants.

The end product of the outside audit is a comprehensive and detailed Auditor's Report, substantiated by a variety of "Exhibits" in the form of "Schedules" and "Reports." These will include schedules of: (1) accounts receivable; (2) statement of inventories; (3) statement of receipts and disbursements; (4) statement of cash flow; (5) statement of assets, liabilities, and net worth; and (6) year-to-year comparisons of growth factors. Frequently, the Annual Report to stockholders is embellished by pictures, graphs, and charts for easy interpretation. An example of this type of reporting is seen in the Annual Report of a domestic corporation shown below.

DISTRIBUTION OF THE INCOME DOLLAR 1962

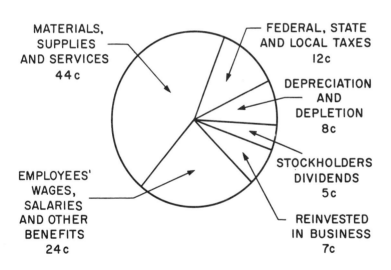

MATERIALS, SUPPLIES AND SERVICES 44c

FEDERAL, STATE AND LOCAL TAXES 12c

DEPRECIATION AND DEPLETION 8c

STOCKHOLDERS DIVIDENDS 5c

EMPLOYEES' WAGES, SALARIES AND OTHER BENEFITS 24c

REINVESTED IN BUSINESS 7c

Here is another point at which the financial operations of the church and commercial enterprises are similar. Let us illustrate the application of graphic representation to church statements by converting the record of expenditures to a pie graph, much like the one used by the commercial enterprise above.

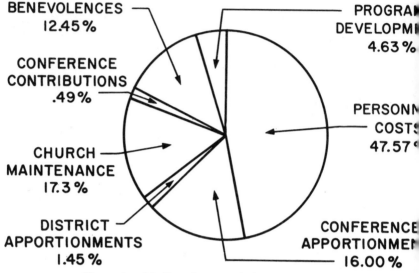

Illustration 30. Distribution of the Income Dollars
for Spring Hill Church, 1963

A Certificate of Audit, setting forth the extent of the examination and the conclusions, is generally required by management and serves either to substantiate or to refute the results of the internal audit and reports. The form and contents of most outside audit reports is represented by the report for Polk Street Methodist Church of Amarillo, Texas. (See Appendix A for complete information as to the coverage of the audit.)

THE PROGRAM AUDIT

There may be a considerable lag in church management's active interest in evaluating *program growth,* deviation from sound practices, and stagnation of leadership as compared with financial need. Whereas discrepancies in the financial records are susceptible to exact quantitative analysis, the factors relating to program performance are largely qualitative and are therefore subjective in nature. Quantitative analyses deal with exact values. Two plus two always equals four and never an approximation. Failure to post one side of a financial transaction always produces an error of an exact amount and one that can be positively identified.

Program audit and analysis are not susceptible to such positive identification. In the first place, checkpoints are sometime rather difficult to establish. Then, units or criteria of measurement are matters of qualitative judgment. Again, there must be a base or point of reckoning with which to compare progress toward the goal. Without a well-defined plan and a progress calendar for each program, it is difficult to determine whether there has been satisfactory progress and whether there has been faithful compliance with or a deviation from the master plan.

PROGRAM PLANNING

It is evident that there should be detailed and specific outlines *in written form* for each program, not for purposes of serving the needs of the auditor but as a guide for daily operations. Of course, there is often great difficulty in securing specific performance in evolving a definitive plan of action for all committees and groups. There is not the authority to compel voluntary workers to follow a specific pattern of operation, nor to produce a blueprint for their programs. This very fact, however, emphasizes one of the fundamental principles of church administration—that achievement inevitably depends upon true leadership, and not upon compulsion externally applied. In a commercial enterprise, compliance can be required by naked authority, but autocratic administration has no rightful place in church management. Under wise and discreet leadership, it is possible to secure the cooperation of most committee and program chairmen in establishing specific objectives and to set up goals of accomplishment.

One approach to securing uniformity is to furnish each committee chairman with a prepared form for his planning sessions with his group. Often it is advisable for someone in central responsibility to meet with each committee in planning sessions prior to the beginning of the new year. Through a series of these sessions, there should evolve a comprehensive schedule of activities and events complete with a progress calendar. It is only against this background that a realistic audit can be made.

Since a high degree of uniformity is necessary for evaluating progress, it is the responsibility of the church administrator or some other designated authority to furnish the chairman with a standard form such as the one illustrated below.

Nearly all functioning groups can define their objectives in some detail. The most important groups, from the standpoint of budget and activities, may include:

1. Music Committee
2. Religious Education
3. Membership and Cultivation
4. Woman's Society
5. Men's Club?
6. Property Committee
7. Food Service—Culinary Committee
8. Missions, Home and Foreign
9. Personnel Committee
10. Finance Commission

Such a list may be expanded to include many more functional groups depending upon the local and denominational situation. An example of identifying and scheduling special events is seen in the operation of the music program. Music for special occasions should be planned weeks and even months in advance of the actual performance. Likewise, the personnel committee will be concerned with discovering and

SPRING HILL CHURCH

Anytown, U. S. A.

PLANNED PROGRAM OF ACTION

1964

The _Junior Choir_ Committee, Commission, or Group

met on _6/2_ 1964; _6/17_ 1964; and _____ 196__

for the purpose of formulating our program of activities for the ensuing year.

Chairman _Joyce Adams_ Vice Chairman _Seth Parker_

Secretary _Beth Samuels_ Treasurer _Sandra Elam_

Sponsor, or Advisor _Mrs. Curtis Hall_

- -

Statement of major purposes: _(1) Build up interest and membership._

(2) Provide opportunities for boys and girls of Spring Hill Church to develop their talents in vocal music.

(3) To learn to sing the hymns of Faith for our enjoyment and to the glory of God.

Calendar of Events: _(1) Sing with Senior Choir three times during the year_

(3) Sing for the 5th Sunday School convocation in August

(4) Perform in the Christmas Pageant

Problems: _(1) Need more boys in our choir_

(2) To find a better time for rehearsals and practice time.

(3) A substitute pianist

File copies with: The Pastor, Director of Religious Education, and Business Manager

Illustration 31. Program Planning Form

developing latent talents of all the members. As previously emphasized failure to explore and develop potential leadership and personality of each member is a mark of incompetence or inexcusable neglect of those in positions of responsibility.

The greatest resource of any church is not in its ability to raise its budget, but in the potential growth and development of its membership. "But as many as receive him, to them gave he *power to become* the sons of God" [St. John I:12].

GLOSSARY

AUDIT. A formal examination of financial records by an auditor, who is authorized to verify and to certify the correctness of the records.

BALANCE. The difference between the debit and credit sides of an account.

BALANCE SHEET. A financial statement showing assets, liabilities, and net worth.

BUDGET. Estimate of available income and a well-though-out plan for spending the money.

BUDGETARY CONTROL. The control of income and expenses by the operation of a budget program. Purpose is to make sure that the various units of the church stay within certain estimates.

CASH. Money in circulation, such as coin and currency, plus certain negotiable instruments, such as checks, drafts, and money orders.

CASHBOOK. A book of original entry that is used for recording all cash received and spent. It may be divided into two separate journals—the Cash Receipts Journal and the Cash Payments Journal.

CONTROLLING ACCOUNT. An account in the General Ledger that shows, in summary form, what appears in detail in the corresponding subsidiary ledge. An example is the accounts receivable controlling account, which shows in summary form the totals of all debits and credits that appear in the Accounts Receivable Ledger.

CREDIT.   The right-hand side of a ledger account.

CURRENCY.   That which is in circulation as a medium of exchange, such as coins, Government notes, and bank notes.

DEBIT (DR.).   (1) The left-hand side of a ledger account. (2) A charge to the left-hand side of an account.

DISCREPANCY.   Failure of accounting records or entries in the books to agree or correspond.

DOUBLE-ENTRY.   A system of bookkeeping employing both debit and credit entries. (Devised by Fra Luca Pacioli, an Italian mathematician, in the late fifteenth century.)

ENTERPRISE.   A business undertaking, for profit, to produce or distribute goods or to render service.

FICA.   Federal Insurance Contributions Act. Sometimes referred to as Old Age Benefit Tax Act (OAB). It is a tax levied on employers and on employees and in certain instances by self-employed persons.

FEDERAL OLD-AGE INSURANCE.   One of the types of benefits under the Federal Social Security Act. It is designed to give individuals covered by its provisions a monthly benefit at the age of 62 for women and at 65 for men. Provision is also made for certain benefits to dependent survivors.

FUNDS.   Sums of money on deposit or set aside for special purposes.

GENERAL JOURNAL.   A book of original entry that may be used in recording all types of business transactions.

JOURNAL.   A book of original entry in which business transactions are recorded in the order of their occurrence.

LEDGER.   Book or record of accounts in the form of a bound book, loose-leaf sheets, or cards which show both debits and credits.

NIGHT DEPOSITORY.   A place for making bank deposits after the bank has closed. Those who pay for the privilege of using this service obtain a key to open a small door in the outside wall of the bank building. The deposit is placed in this special receptical.

PETTY CASH. A fund set up to make small payments, such as those for car fare, messenger service, and postage due.

PURCHASE REQUISITION. A request that a purchasing department in a business receives from another department needing equipment, materials, or supplies.

SORTER. (1) In filing, it is a series of boxes or locations into which papers are placed so as to arrange them in alphabetical order. (2) In data processing, it is a machine that places cards in the proper passage, pocket, or slot according to the location of a given hole in the slot.

SUBSCRIBE. To agree with, or give support to, a principle in which one believes.

TELLER. One who receives and pays out money, or one who counts money.

TRUSTEE. A person holding in trust the property of another.

VOUCHER. An instrument, such as a receipt or a canceled check, that is legal evidence of the transfer of money in a business transaction.

WORK FLOW. The systematic route by which work passes from one process to another; often shown by means of special *flow charts*.

BIBLIOGRAPHY

BRAMER, JOHN C. JR. *Efficient Church Business Management.* Philadelphia: The Westminster Press, 1960.

CANNON, A. M. "Financial Statements for a Church." *The Journal of Accountancy,* September, 1962.

HOLCK, MANFRED. *Accounting for a Small Church.* Minneapolis: The Augsburg Press, 1961.

HOLT, DAVID R. *Handbook for Church Finance.* New York: The Macmillan Company, 1960.

KAHN, GILBERT; YEARIN, THEODORE; and STEWART, JEFFREY. *Progressive Filing.* New York: The Gregg Publishing Division, McGraw-Hill Book Company, 1961.

LEACH, WILLIAM H. *Handbook for Church Management.* Englewood Cliffs, N.J.: Prentice-Hall, 1958.

LEVIN, HOWARD S. *Office Work and Automation.* New York: John Wiley and Sons, 1956.

PAGE, HARRY R. *Church Budget Development.* Englewood Cliffs, N.J.: Prentice-Hall, 1964.

SELDEN, WILLIAM; and NANNASSY, LOUIS C. *Business Dictionary.* Englewood Cliffs, N.J.: Prentice-Hall, 1960.

SELDEN, WILLIAM; STRAUB, LAURA L.; and PORTER, LEONARD J. *Filing and Finding.* Englewood Cliffs, N.J.: Prentice-Hall, 1962.

SHERWOOD, J. F.; CARSON, A. B.; and BOLING, CLEM. *College Accounting.* Cincinnati, Ohio: South-Western Publishing Company, 1957.

STREUFERT, E. R., and RAUSCHER, R. C. *Fund Accounting Systems for Churches.* St. Louis, Mo.: The Lutheran Church—Missouri Synod, 1958.

TERRY, GEORGE R. *Principles of Management.* Homewood, Illinois: Richard D. Irwin, 1956.

Introduction to Data Processing. New York: Haskins & Sells, 1960.

Financial Principles and Procedures for the Local Church. ——— ———; Department of the Budget and Finance, The United Presbyterian Church in the U.S.A., 1962.

Complete Auditor's Report

POLK STREET METHODIST CHURCH

Amarillo, Texas

From November 1, 1960, through October 31, 1961

AUDITOR'S REPORT

MANNING HOLLAND
Certified Public Accountant

MANNING HOLLAND
Certified Public Accountant
313 W. 15th
Amarillo, Texas

December 13, 1961

Commission on Stewardship and Finance
Polk Street Methodist Church
Amarillo, Texas

Gentlemen:

In accordance with your request, we have made an audit of the books and records of the Polk Street Methodist Church in Amarillo, Texas, for the period from November 1, 1960 through October 31, 1961. This report includes the following as resulted from cash transactions:

(1) Exhibit A—   Balance Sheet as of October 31, 1961, page 1.

(2) Exhibit B—   Comparison of Regular Fund Cash Receipts and Disbursements with Budget from November 1, 1960, through October 31, 1961, page 2.

(3) Exhibit C—   Comparative Regular Fund Cash Receipts and Disbursements for fiscal years ending October 31, 1961 and 1960, page 3.

(4) Exhibit D—   Cash Receipts and Disbursements of Special Fund from November 1, 1960, through October 31, 1961, page 4.

(5) Exhibit E—   Comparative Cash Receipts and Disbursements of Kitchen Fund for fiscal years ending October 31, 1961 and 1960, page 5.

(6) Schedule A—   Bank Reconciliation of Regular Fund as of October 31, 1961, page 6.

(7) Schedule B—   Bank Reconciliation of Special Fund as of October 31, 1961, page 7.

(8) Schedule C—   Bank Reconciliation of Kitchen Fund as of October 31, 1961, page 8.

(9) Comments—   Pages 9 through 11.

Our examination was made in accordance with generally accepted auditing standards, and accordingly included such test of the accounting records and such other auditing procedures as we considered necessary in the circumstances.

In our opinion, the accompanying balance sheet, cash receipts, and disbursements present fairly the financial position of the Polk Street Methodist Church as of October 31, 1961, and the results of operation on a cash basis, for the fiscal year then ended, on a basis consistent with that of the preceding year.

Yours truly,

(Authorized Copy)

Manning Holland

POLK STREET METHODIST CHURCH

Amarillo, Texas

From November 1, 1960, through October 31, 1961

AUDITOR'S REPORT

MANNING HOLLAND
Certified Public Accountant

POLK STREET METHODIST CHURCH
Balance Sheet
As of October 31, 1961

ASSETS

Current Assets

Cash		$ 12,868.38

Fixed Assets

Land—cost	$128,625.00	
Parsonage and church building—cost	899,215.01	
Furnishings and equipment—appraised	170,100.00	
Total fixed assets		1,197,940.01
Total assets		$1,210,808.39

LIABILITIES AND NET WORTH

Liabilities

Note payable—bank		$ 113,075.00

Net Worth

Unappropriated surplus		1,097,733.39
Total liabilities and net worth		$1,210,808.39

Note

As the church is operating on a cash basis, the unpaid pledges are not included in this Exhibit.

– 1 –

POLK STREET METHODIST CHURCH

Comparison of Regular Fund Cash Receipts and Disbursements with Budget

From November 1, 1960, thru October 31, 1961

	Cash	Budget	Increase (Decrease)
Cash on hand—November 1, 1960	$ 849.78	$ –0–	$ 849.78
Receipts:			
Previous fiscal year pledges	4,106.15	–0–	4,106.15
Current fiscal year pledges	242,443.06	256,116.40	(13,673.34)
Plate collections	8,251.43	–0–	8,251.43
Easter collection	5,712.18	–0–	5,712.18
Total receipts	260,512.82	256,116.40	4,396.42
Total cash available	261,362.60	256,116.40	5,246.20
Budget Disbursements:			
Ministerial support	26,372.50	33,550.00	(7,177.50)
Connectional obligations	7,813.36	9,161.00	(1,347.64)
Administrative salaries	24,143.19	23,850.00	293.19
Administrational and general expenses	27,219.58	26,900.00	319.58
Benevolences	71,936.45	72,721.00	(784.55)
Music and choir	13,173.68	13,150.00	23.68
Membership and evangelism	2,471.17	1,930.00	541.17
Church school	19,266.85	20,270.00	(1,003.15)
Building and grounds engineers, janitors, etc.	18,252.94	18,886.00	(633.06)
Commission on Christian social relations	60.25	250.00	(189.75)
Utilities and elevators service	7,530.66	8,205.00	(674.34)
Repairs to building and equipment	9,666.97	8,750.00	916.97
Kitchen expenses	6,049.32	5,931.00	118.32
Insurance	3,620.39	4,000.00	(379.61)
Debt retirement—note payment	13,681.77	12,681.77	1,000.00
Debt retirement—interest expense	8,933.07	6,337.84	2,595.23
Total budget disbursements	260,192.15	266,573.61	(6,381.46)
Other Disbursements:			
Previous fiscal year expenses	1,208.73	–0–	1,208.73
Total disbursements	261,400.88	266,573.61	(5,172.73)
Cash on hand—October 31, 1961	$ (38.28)	$ (10,457.21)	$ 10,418.93

– 2 –

Exhibit C

POLK STREET METHODIST CHURCH
Comparative Regular Fund Cash Receipts and Disbursements
For Fiscal Years Ending October 31, 1961 and 1960

	October 31 1961	October 31 1960	Increase (Decrease)
Cash on hand—Beginning balance	$ 849.78	$ 13,425.73	$(12,575.95)
Receipts:			
Previous fiscal year pledges	4,106.15	6,274.96	(2,168.81)
Current fiscal year pledges	242,443.06	244,466.78	(2,023.72)
Plate collections	8,251.43	8,803.02	(551.59)
Easter collection	5,712.18	7,869.81	(2,157.63)
Bank loan for operating expense	–0–	9,000.00	(9,000.00)
Bank loan for air conditioner	–0–	126,756.77	(126,756.77)
Total receipts	260,512.82	403,171.34	(142,658.52)
Total cash available	261,362.60	416,597.07	(155,234.47)
Budget Disbursements:			
Ministerial support	26,372.50	27,203.97	(831.47)
Connectional obligations	7,813.36	8,507.33	(693.97)
Administrative salaries	24,143.19	26,220.60	(2,077.41)
Administrational and general expenses	27,219.58	32,781.10	(5,561.52)
Benevolences	71,936.45	67,079.91	4,856.54
Music and choir	13,173.68	12,972.45	201.23
Membership and evangelism	2,471.17	1,927.95	543.22
Church school	19,266.85	23,239.96	(3,973.11)
Building and grounds engineer, janitors, etc.	18,252.94	19,060.89	(807.95)
Commission on Christian social relations	60.25	188.80	(128.55)
Utilities and elevators	7,530.66	7,570.76	(40.10)
Repairs to building and equipment	9,666.97	7,746.63	1,920.34
Kitchen expense	6,049.32	5,626.16	423.16
Insurance	3,620.39	6,376.18	(2,755.79)
Redecoration expense	–0–	14,628.19	(14,628.19)
Debt retirement—note payments	13,681.77	–0–	13,681.77
Debt retirement—interest expense	8,933.07	–0–	8,933.07
Total budget disbursements	260,192.15	261,130.88	(938.73)
Other Disbursements:			
Previous fiscal year expenses	1,208.73	301.81	906.92
Air-conditioner cost	–0–	126,756.77	(126,756.77)
Bank loan payment	–0–	27,000.00	(27,000.00)
Bank loan interest expense	–0–	557.83	(557.83)
Total other disbursements	1,208.73	154,616.41	(153,407.68)
Total disbursements	261,400.88	415,747.29	(154,346.41)
Cash on hand—Ending balance	$ (38.28)	$ 849.78	$ (888.06)

Polk Street Methodist Church

Cash Receipts and Disbursements of Special Fund

From November 1, 1960, thru October 31, 1961

Cash on hand—November 1, 1960		$ 8,806.26
Receipts:		
1960–1961 fiscal year pledges	$ 175.00	
1961–1962 fiscal year pledges	7,119.50	
Junior–Senior High department	263.27	
Methodist home at Waco, Texas	6,077.76	
Benevolences	1,827.94	
Equipment replacement and repairs	6,302.26	
Expense refund	9,413.36	
Joyce Hill Fund	185.10	
Africa Special	1,131.87	
Mexican Mission	605.13	
Chapel Singers	1,245.16	
Easter fund	364.10	
Day Kindergarten	1,993.68	
Choir bells	209.42	
Childrens division	452.85	
Miscellaneous projects	1,253.50	
Total receipts		38,619.90
Total cash available		47,426.16
Disbursements:		
1960–1961 fiscal year pledges	6,712.25	
Junior–Senior High department	188.52	
Methodist home at Waco, Texas	5,887.26	
Benevolences	766.44	
Equipment replacement and repairs	5,984.38	
Expense refunds	9,413.73	
Joyce Hill Fund	185.10	
Africa Special	1,131.87	
Mexican Mission	107.63	
Chapel Singers	1,499.03	
Easter fund	371.00	
Day Kindergarten	1,584.75	
Choir bells	246.92	
Childrens division	542.64	
Miscellaneous projects	1,254.76	
Total disbursements		35,876.28
Cash on hand—October 31, 1961		$11,549.88

— 4 —

Polk Street Methodist Church
Comparative Cash Receipts and Disbursements of
Kitchen Fund

For Fiscal Years Ending October 31, 1961 and 1960

	October 31 1961	October 31 1960	Increase (Decrease)
Cash on hand—Beginning balance	$ 517.50	$ 1,192.68	$ (675.18)
Receipts:			
Men's breakfast	489.67	534.70	(45.03)
Family night	2,274.05	1,374.80	899.25
Evangelism luncheons	735.35	485.40	249.95
Quarterly conference	–0–	125.00	(125.00)
Teachers' luncheons	126.00	474.00	(348.00)
Regular services paid by church	10,804.48	7,187.82	3,616.66
Regular services paid by others	1,493.96	2,733.12	(1,239.16)
Minister's luncheon	28.50	375.34	(346.84)
Slater reception	–0–	149.03	(149.03)
Thanksgiving dinner	–0–	215.10	(215.10)
Boy Scouts' dinner	–0–	247.50	(247.50)
Annual conference	–0–	389.68	(389.68)
Servicemen's dinners	649.44	–0–	649.44
Previous year expense refund— cancelled check	4.00	–0–	4.00
Total receipts	16,605.45	14,291.49	2,313.96
Total cash available	17,122.95	15,484.17	1,638.78
Disbursements:			
Food	11,332.23	10,647.22	685.01
Labor	2,797.75	2,643.35	154.40
Supplies	530.08	739.13	(209.05)
Laundry	136.36	132.30	4.06
Cash change	675.00	545.00	130.00
Group refunds	154.75	248.42	(93.67)
Returned checks (unsigned)	–0–	11.25	(11.25)
Equipment—freezer payments	140.00	–0–	140.00
Total disbursements	15,766.17	14,966.67	799.50
Cash on hand—Ending balance	$ 1,356.78	$ 517.50	$ 839.28

– 5 –

Polk Street Methodist Church
Bank Reconciliation of Regular Fund
As of October 31, 1961

Balance per Bank Statement				$15,382.11

Add Deposits in Transit:

	Date	Amount	
	10–31–61	$ 723.00	
	10–31–6	5.00	
Total deposits in transit			728.00
			16,110.11

Less Outstanding Checks:

Check Number	Amount	Check Number	Amount
2558	$ 75.00	3100	$ 8.00
3039	424.20	3101	710.22
3055	25.19	3102	3,849.87
3079	6.65	3101	5.31
3081	125.00	3592	118.91
3082	1,041.00	3593	44.38
3083	83.00	3595	98.55
3085	43.00	3597	60.10
3086	3,895.24	3598	60.10
3087	59.97	3601	175.00
3094	250.00	3602	123.62
3095	4.00	3603	103.55
3096	231.00	3604	204.99
3097	8.00	3605	84.22
3098	4.00	3606	119.47
3099	4,000.00	3607	106.85

Total outstanding checks		16,148.39
Balance per Books		$ (38.28)

– 6 –

POLK STREET METHODIST CHURCH
Bank Reconciliation of Special Fund
As of October 31, 1961

Balance per Bank Statement	$11,546.88
Add Deposit in Transit: October 31, 1961	8.00
	11,554.88
Less Outstanding Check: Number 861	5.00
Balance per Books	$11,549.88

POLK STREET METHODIST CHURCH
Bank Reconciliation of Kitchen Fund
As of October 31, 1961

Balance per Bank Statement $ 731.25

Add Deposits in Transit:

Date	Amount	
10–31–61	$710.22	
10–31–61	5.31	
Total deposits in transit		715.53
		1,446.78

Less Outstanding Checks:

Check Number	Amount	
3329	13.53	
3340	18.50	
3341	8.50	
3342	7.50	
3343	17.00	
3344	19.00	
3345	5.97	
Total outstanding checks		90.00
Balance per Books		$1,356.78

– 7 –

COMMENTS

These comments supplement the financial statements.

HISTORY AND ORGANIZATION

The Polk Street Methodist Church was organized November 23, 1888, as a Methodist Church of the Northwest Texas Conference of Methodist Churches. Since then, this church has grown to be the largest Methodist Church in Amarillo, Texas, and one of the larger churches of the conference.

BALANCE SHEET

Exhibit A, page 1, presents the assets and liabilities.

Current Assets—$12,868.38

We sent a standard bank confirmation form to the church depository's bank and reconciled the amount they showed to the records. Schedule A, page 6, shows the bank reconciliation of the regular fund as of October 31, 1961. Schedule B, page 7, and Schedule C, page 8, presents the bank reconciliation of the special and kitchen funds for period ending October 31, 1961. The cancelled checks and deposits were test checked to the books as deemed necessary. The bank balances of the three funds are:

Regular fund	$ (38.28)
Special fund	11,549.88
Kitchen fund	1,356.78
Total bank balances	$12,868.38

Fixed Assets—$1,197,940.01

We tried to determine the actual cost of the church land and buildings from records and information obtainable. No allowance was made for depreciation or obsolescence.

Land costs for the following:

Church building and parsonage	$ 64,250.00
Annex church building and parsonage	45,900.00
Corner lots acquired in 1959	18,475.00
Total land cost	$128,625.00

— 8 —

Parsonage and church building costs:

Parsonage	$ 26,649.00
Church	362,996.07
Organ	17,450.00
Annex	365,363.17
Air conditioner	126,756.77
Total parsonage and building costs	$899,215.01

As the records of the prior years were stored in various places of the church by various people, the cost of the furnishings and equipment on hand could not be easily verified. We used the appraised value of the furnishings and equipment as approved by the Fourth Quarterly Conference of May 9, 1961, prepared by the church Board of Trustees for insurance coverage. Of the $170,100,00 appraised value, $10,000.00 is for furnishings in the parsonage.

Liabilities—$113,075.00

In order for the church to install the church air conditioner, the Board of Stewards approved the borrowing of money to finance the cost. A 5% annual installment note, amounting to $126,756.77, dated May 18, 1960, due May 18, 1965, was given to the Amarillo National Bank. The annual installment for each year is as follows:

	Original Note	Note Balance
May 18, 1961 for	$ 12,681.77	
May 18, 1962 for	12,675.00	$ 11,675.00
May 18, 1963 for	12,675.00	12,675.00
May 18, 1964 for	12,675.00	12,675.00
May 18, 1965 for	76,050.00	76,050.00
Total payments	$126,756.77	$113,075.00

The first interest payment was due May 18, 1961. Then semi-annual interest payments will be due each November 18 and May 18, until the note is paid in full.

Net Worth—$1,097,733.39

The unappropriated surplus amounting to $1,097,733.39 is the difference between the total assets of $1,210,808.39 and the current liabilities of $113,075.00.

OPERATION

A summary of operation is shown in Exhibits B, C, D, and E.

In Exhibit B, page 2, it may be seen that the budget for the fiscal year ending October 31, 1961, amounted to $266,573.61. Yet the total pledges amounted to $256.116.40. The pledges were $10,457.21 short of the budget. Though the total receipts amounted to $260,512.82, $4,106.15 was prior fiscal year pledges. Therefore the receipts for the current fiscal year amounted to $256,406.67. The budget disbursements were trimmed to $260,-192.15, which amounts to $3,785.48 more than the current fiscal year receipts of $256,406.67. The fiscal year pledge receipts of $242,443.06 were $13,673.34 short of the total fiscal year pledges, amounting to $256,116.40. Cash on hand as of October 31, 1961, amounting to $(38.28) decreased $888.06 under balance of $849.78 on hand November 1, 1960.

Exhibit C, page 3, shows a comparison of the regular fund cash receipts and disbursements for the fiscal years ending October 31, 1961 and 1960. The total pledges received for each year are as follows:

	October 31	
	1961	1960
Current fiscal year pledges	$242,443.06	$244,466.78
Previous year pledges after October 31, 1960	–0–	4,106.15
Previous year pledges received in November and December, 1961 to date of this report	2,981.15	–0–
Total pledges received for each year	$245,424.21	$248,572.93

The difference in totals between the years amounts to $3,148.72. As may be seen in Exhibit C, page 3, the budget disbursements for the year ending October 31, 1960, exceeded the budget disbursements for the year ending October 31, 1961, in the amount of $938.73.

The special fund is used to handle the various church receipts and disbursements that do not pertain to the budget or kitchen activities. Exhibit D, page 4, reflects the receipts and disbursements of this fund for the fiscal year ending October 31, 1961.

– 10 –

The 1961-1962 fiscal year pledge of $7,119.50 was transferred to the regular fund in the first week of November, 1961.

A kitchen fund was set up separately from the regular fund to handle the kitchen operation. Exhibit E, page 5, shows that the disbursements of $15,766.17 were $839.58 less than the receipts of $16,605.45 for the period ending October 31, 1961. Yet the following kitchen workers salaries were paid through the budget disbursements of the regular fund.

Hostess	$3,042.50
Regular maid	2,348.32
Extra maid	658.50
Total	$6,049.32

So the actual kitchen disbursements for the period would amount to $21,815.49 as follows:

Disbursement as per Exhibit D	$15,766.17
Salaries paid through regular fund	6,049.32
Total kitchen operations disbursements	$21,815.49

This total disbursement of $21,815.49 exceeds the receipts of $16.605.45 by $5,210.04. We understand that the reason the receipts are short of the disbursements is due to the fact that in charging for the meals served through the kitchen all the labor cost is not considered. Therefore the people who pay for their meals are not paying the actual cost of such meals.

Study and Teaching Suggestions

SUGGESTIONS FOR LEADERS AND MEMBERS
OF STUDY GROUPS

If you want to be an effective leader or member of an adult study group, you must understand that the members of your group have certain definite needs and interests. Otherwise they would not be present!

You will know also that these interests and needs must be the basis for the leader's objectives and will find expression through his instructional plans and procedures. Only through alert recognition of the personal motives of the members, and through the wise use of group dynamics, can these needs be most effectively met.

Some Facts to Keep in Mind:

1. Those who make up this group come from many churches, which means each has a different background with many and varied interests.

2. Each person has come for some specific reason and has his own need that he is seeking to fulfill.

3. Each person is interested in why others are in the group, where they are from, and what position they hold in their church. Provision should be made, even if only during a break, for this information to become known.

4. Each person wants to know what subject matter is to be covered and what is expected of him.

5. Each person in the group wants to know the sources of help both from reading material and from others in the group.

6. Each person needs to know that he is accepted as a member of the group. He needs to be heard from as well as to hear from others in the group.

7. Some persons may have fears that the group will be above or below their interests and knowledge.

8. Each person needs to participate in solving problems that are presented. He needs to know that he, and every other person in the group, may make contributions that are distinctly his own.

9. Each person in the group needs to be stimulated mentally and spiritually during each session of the course.

10. Every person in the group should be helped to feel that he is glad he came, even if in the beginning he was not quite sure why.

The Leadership Role:

1. The good leader regards the class as an opportunity for creating situations in which group members themselves make significant decisions, solve important problems, implement programs, and pay witness to their faith in God.

2. The good leader will help each person to become involved in the activity of the group and thereby share his knowledge with others.

3. The good leader will make it self-evident that this is a Christian study group.

4. There will be a clear understanding that church officials need to have basic knowledge about finance, accountancy, business management, and economics in order to promote the temporal welfare of the church.

5. The good leader will be skillful in making each member know that he is accepted as an important part of the group and that he is expected to participate in solving of the problems presented.

6. There will be continual recognition that the members of the group differ in theological beliefs, denominational loyalties, congregational practices, educational achievements, life experiences, racial and social backgrounds, physical capacities, and psychological reactions.

7. At the completion of each session each member should feel a sense of fulfillment, of having made significant decisions, of having solved important problems, and of having witnessed to his faith in God.

An Overview:

In reference to this course in Church Accounting Methods, certain basic (A) premises, (B) problems and (C) questions may be raised that will serve as guidelines for the several succeeding sessions.

A. Major Premises:

1. If churches are to carry out their mission effectively, their business affairs must be managed as competently as those of other organizations.

2. Because churches are service-producing rather than profit-making institutions, their accounting procedures will differ in some ways from those of commercial businesses, and these differences must be identified.

3. The task of accounting for income and expenditures of the church is a basic function of Christian stewardship.

4. Accounting for and to members on their individual financial commitments is a primary service of church business management.

B. Major Problems:

1. How to devise an accounting system that will be efficient, economical and responsive to all the needs of the church.

2. How to account for nonoperating income and expenditures without comingling funds with the "operating" accounts.

3. How to handle cash receipts with dispatch and under good security.

4. What kinds of periodic reports to issue, to whom, and at what time intervals.

5. How to report the total financial and service programs of the church in the absence of a truly "unified budget" operation.

6. How to determine whether the accounting system is a consequence of the budget structure, or vice versa, and why.

7. When to employ full manual, posting machine method, or electronic data processing procedures in church accounting practices.

8. How to coordinate the Chart of Accounts and related activities with records control and office filing system.

9. What kind of outside audit service to employ and at what time interval.

10. How to handle asset, liability and other "trustee" accounts.

C. *Pertinent and Persistent Questions:*

1. How does adequate stewardship of financial records facilitate church planning for: (a) seasonal fluctuations in receipts; (b) periodic major expenditures; (c) benevolences and outreach programs; (d) denominational apportionments; and (e) comparative fiscal reporting?

2. In what respects do accounting and reporting procedures based on a "unified budget" differ from accounting and reporting for a diversified series of department or unit budgets?

3. Why, how, and by whom should inventories be kept of: (a) physical properties; (b) notes and mortgages; (c) investment certificates?

4. What particular relationships should exist between the church's accounting records and its total system of records maintenance?

5. To whom, by whom, and for what purposes should financial reports be made?

6. By whom and for what purposes should an annual audit be made of the church's financial records?

7. Would your church's definition of an audit be acceptable to professional accountants? Why?

8. What are some specific responsibilities and duties of the following in relation to church accounting and reporting: pastor, lay leader, board chairman, treasurer, trustees, financial secretary, director of religious education, business manager?

9. What have been some significant developments or trends in church accounting and reporting during the past 20 years?

10. What innovations in church accounting do you predict for the next 10 years?

11. How are budget estimates of receipts and expenditures recorded in books of account?

12. Of what use is a chart of Cash Flow? How is it constructed?

13. To what extent should special columns be used in a Multicolumnar Cash Journal?

14. How are transactions entered for accounts not having a "special" column in the Multicolumnar Cash Journal?

15. What is the criterion for establishing a ledger account for specific items of receipts and expenditures?

16. Which church official is primarily responsible for determining the organization of the accounting system in churches not having a business manager?

17. What is "Fund Accounting"? For what are "funds" credited, and for what are they debited?

18. How do "funds" appear on the balance sheet?

19. What are the advantages of using a three-column "balance" ledger form?

20. What documents validate requests for replenishment of the petty cash account?

CHAPTER 1. THE PURPOSES OF CHURCH ACCOUNTING

A clear understanding of the nature and purpose of an account is necessary to a working knowledge of keeping systematic records of assets, liabilities, income, and expenses. Visual and action devices with which to illustrate the effect of balance in an account include the "T" diagram, the teeter-totter, and the postal scales.

The knowledge that for every debit in one account there is an equal and corresponding credit value in another account helps establish the principle of continuous equality of total debits with total credits. The discussion leader will find an abundance of materials and methods for illustrating this fundamental fact. One of the most effective and immediately available means is through the use of several appropriate "T" accounts with cash, income, and expense. Half dozen routine transactions properly entered on debit and credit sides of appropriate accounts will suffice.

The use of the ledger ruling as a way of classifying assets, income, and expenses into "accounts" is a first step toward the concept of organizing financial facts into a system. It is helpful to exhibit both forms of the ledger shown on page 17 —one that must be "calculated" in order to find the "balance" and the other that continuously shows the amount of the balance.

The periodic report of operations, such as is shown in part on page 20, emphasizes the effect of transactions on the various budget accounts and the importance of knowing the amount of "balance" or deficit in an account. The value of balance or equality can be effectively illustrated by observing the relationship of the amount shown in Column 1 with the amounts in Columns 4 and 6.

Constructive implementation of this discussion on the purposes of church accounting can be provided by a problem of recording the transactions for a month or a week into the correct account and at the end of the problem testing for equality of total debits with total credits. For example: show on a blackboard, or by the use of a prepared chart, "T" accounts for:

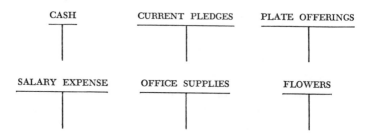

Record in these accounts these transactions with cash:
a. Received $600 from *current pledges.*
b. Received $45 from *plate offerings.*
c. Paid $400 for *Salaries.*
d. Paid $5 for *Office Supplies.*
e. Received $10 for *flowers.*
f. Paid $7.50 for altar *flowers.*

The equality of debits and credits may be tested after any of these transactions and the end of the problem.

Each of the four *preview* questions at the beginning of this chapter is a fruitful source for group discussion.

Teaching Suggestions

CHAPTER 2. TYPES OF ACCOUNTING SYSTEMS

The key word and idea in this discussion is *system.* It is supremely important that the persons responsible for keeping church records understand the necessity for order and system in maintaining them—that only through the consistent use of systematic procedures can the financial facts be helpful in planning and conducting the temporal affairs of the church.

Introduction of the so-called "single-entry system" is for the sole purpose of dramatizing its inadequacies. Only in very small situations will there be a place for the memorandum procedure. Its shortcomings in most churches are readily discernible in the example given on page 25 and in the questions. Time consumed by the group in arriving at the answers to these questions may be used to thoroughly condemn the "single-entry system" of keeping financial records. It is readily seen that related facts are very difficult to summarize from simple chronological listings. The degree of inefficiency becomes clear when the same transactions are shown classified on the multicolumnar journal that provides also for simultaneous recording of both debit and credit for each transaction.

Although the one principal purpose of this course is to emphasize the desirability of providing an *adequate* system and procedures for accounting for all sizes of churches, a note of caution needs to be raised lest there develop excesses of overorganization. Condemnation of single entry should not lead to the adoption of a double-entry system that is too complex for the nature and volume of transactions to be handled. It is fundamental that the *system* fit the *situation*, and to achieve a proper fit the starting point is a careful study and analysis of the *situation*.

Devising, adopting, or adapting a *system* is the second step and not the first. What is required as a result of an analytical study will find its place in one of the following list of ascending complexities: (1) a memorandum only; (2) a Multicolumnar Cash Journal with voucher file; (3) a complete set of books of original and final entry, hand kept; (4) a machine system; or (5) electronic data processing system.

Particular stress should be placed on the necessity of placing responsibility for authorizing expenditures and purchases. Without built-in controls such as the voucher system, indecision, inefficiency, and misunderstandings often result. Many illustrations can be made by real or hypothetical cases.

Make certain that the three *preview* questions have been thoroughly explored.

CHAPTER 3. ACCOUNTING TO WHOM AND FOR WHAT?

The church accountant or bookkeeper, as the case may be, is responsible for maintaining an accurate and revealing system of records of financial transactions entrusted to him. Obviously, his records will be only as complete as the information channeled to him. In many churches, only a portion of the total volume of financial data is given to the bookkeeper, this resulting in incomplete financial records on a unified basis.

This is a salient point for discussion. What are the pros and cons of the unified system? How does it contrast with the departmental or diversified system? The discussion leader may stimulate thinking on this problem by adopting a particular point of view—for example, one favoring a departmental budgetary and accounting procedure for: the church school; women's organization; youth group; and other affiliated organizations, on the premise that largely autonomous financial status stimulates leadership development and results in a deeper stewardship commitment. On the other hand, an equally good case can be made for a highly unified approach because it exemplifies oneness of purpose throughout the congregation. Here is a fine opportunity for organizing the group into differing schools of thought and debating the values of the two points of view. This is group dynamics in action.

The problem of accounting for and reporting to individual membership on the status of gifts is one of the most sensitive areas of church accounting. There are numerous methods and procedures in this field of activity—enough variations to furnish "talking" material for two or more groups.

Thorough discussion of the three preview questions will be relevant to the suggestions for developing the subject title of the chapter.

CHAPTER 4. WHO KEEPS THE BOOKS OF ACCOUNTS

The purposes of this discussion are to identify the qualifications of the church bookkeeper and to determine the physical properties involved.

Record keeping for most churches requires only moderate skills in the handling of financial information, provided, however, that a good system has already been installed. Recording receipts and expenditures in the appropriate accounts may be largely a matter of knowing the system and the ability to read instructions and make simple analyses of transactions.

The discussion group can easily enumerate a number of personality qualities as requisites to success on the job. Among them are: neatness in dress and handwriting; accuracy in reading and computation; attention to details; conscientiousness; promptness in handling papers; the ability to turn out work; a sense of humor; and some knowledge of accounting principles and procedures.

Attention should be focused on the desirable physical requirements of the office in which the record keeping will be done. There will be considerable opportunity for exploring the space requirements, minimal needs for equipment and supplies, and the extent to which automated processes may be applied.

Creative effort can be stimulated by allowing each member to try his hand at designing an office such as is shown on page 47 of the book. Another individual or group effort may be stimulated by a study of the capabilities of various computing, duplicating and bookkeeping machines. A third project can be built around the best type of filing system and method of records control.

CHAPTER 5. THE RELATIONSHIP OF ACCOUNTING TO BUDGETARY ADMINISTRATION

An interesting question is whether the format and line items of the budget document grows out of the accounting system, or vice versa. There will be those who will appropriately contend that the budget is developed from a descriptive statement of the church's program and that the accounts are constructed to reflect adequately the inflow of receipts and the outgo of expenditures. Therefore, they say, "the accounting system is a child of rather than a parent to the budget document."

This is a fundamental point. The accounting system is essentially a statement of the philosophy of the mission of the church over an indefinite period of operation, whereas the budget expresses the motives and missions for a year or less—subject of course to readoption. Both are instruments of control. Both may be said to "define policy, define objectives, and delineate programs."

An interesting and informative discussion can develop from the "how" and "wherein" applied to each of these three characteristics of the accounting system. In what section of the Chart of Accounts is operating policy defined? What sections express objectives? And wherein is the program of the church delineated? Apply these three questions to the Asset Section; Liability Section; Income Section; Operating Expenses; Benevolences; and Capital Improvement.

Steps in the development of the budget provides an insight into the effectiveness of fiscal planning or the lack of it. How does it take shape? What determines the inclusion or exclusion of any particular line item? What does a line item of $3,600 "Miscellaneous Expenses" tell us concerning the lack of efficiency of the budgeting and accounting procedure?

The design of the system of accounts must be such that periodic statements of current financial status and comparative positions with previous periods of operations can be readily available. To what extent does the lack of such availability adversely affect management controls? Criticize the facsimile copy of the Statement of Operating Income and Expenses in Illustration 17. What information is of little or no use in the statement? What useful information is lacking or incomplete? How would you propose to improve either the format or the content, or both?

CHAPTER 6. ACCOUNTING FOR RECEIPTS

Handling the cash receipts presents one of the most exacting and persistent problems in church financial administration. In fairness to the individual and for the protection to the church, there should be strict observance of these basic rules:

1. No one person is allowed to count and deposit cash without the benefit of having a second one witness it.

2. The same person is never asked to handle cash and to originate the records of accounting without the protection of an authorized witness who countersigns the records.

3. Cash receipts are verified and deposited at the earliest practicable time following collection, whether from congregational offering or by mail.

4. All payments (except petty cash) are made by check.

5. Receipts are required for all cash entrusted to others and received from others.

Each of these statements may be subjected to group discussion in order to bring out the reasons behind them.

Procedures for handling the offering will quite naturally differ from one church to another. It will be both interesting and helpful to have three or four members of your group prepare detailed descriptions of the procedures that are followed in their respective churches and to defend their cases against the criticisms of the group.

Forms for recording receipts and making transfers and deposits are necessary in handling cash. Those illustrated in the text suggest one good approach. The class should have the opportunity of describing and illustrating with sample forms "better methods."

Many persons in church administration are genuinely concerned about the practice in some churches where "inside" officials manipulate secret or hidden funds. To what extent should the pastor or other officials withhold funds from the accounting records and administer them without the knowledge of the congregation? Can such practice be justified on any basis and to any degree? Under what circumstances would you condone it?

A strong case is made in the chapter for the employment of a church business manager or church administrator for many more churches than now have such an official. What are the criteria for employing a full-time business manager; a part-time business manager? Review the elements of the Job Description and have the group justify each of the suggested duties and responsibilities.

CHAPTER 7. ACCOUNTING FOR DISBURSEMENTS

Key points in this chapter relate to the authorization for expenditures and obligations. The use and abuse of the Petty Cash Fund is susceptible to discussion. Then, there is the problem of recording disbursements in a manner that will facilitate quick and accurate reporting. The use of the voucher as a means of controlling expenditures and commitments constitutes another topic of high relevance. All these methods and procedures may be highlighted by exhibits and demonstrations of the forms and records involved. Each member of the group can be a "working" member by assigning each the task of collecting as much material as possible to bring to the class for this discussion.

The columnar journal is suggested as an economical means of classifying both income and expenditures. There are limitations, of course. The Chart of Accounts in illustration 21 may form the basis for defining the maximum usefulness of the columnar journal and for classifying and controlling expenses. Which of the budget items (a) must, (b) could, and (c) should not be included in the Multicolumnar Cash Journal with a separate column? Why do the "fund" accounts show debit balances? Is it because they are "reserves" for the section of the ledger that they support? If no checks are drawn directly on these accounts, how is money finally paid?

Some discussion may be held on the subject of the sequence arrangement of the various categories of receipts and disbursements in the Multicolumnar Cash Journal. How is posting made from the special columns? What kind of transactions are recorded in the "General Ledger" column? Why? Why is it necessary to handle certain nonoperating funds through the "Received and Disbursements" column?

Each member may be assigned to design a multicolumnar journal—real or hypothetical—for use in his church.

CHAPTER 8. HOW TO PLAN FOR CHURCH ACCOUNTING

Planning and designing a system of accounts will require an intimate knowledge of the organizational structure and program objectives of the particular church. Therefore, it is necessary to begin a discussion of this problem by analyzing and interpreting the needs as they are expressed in the various phases of work.

First, we might list the potential sources of income on a blackboard and then explore each as to the probable volume and appropriateness of appeal. For example: what is the attitude of the class toward the annual or periodic Every Member Canvass? What is the place, if any, of church dinners as a fund-raising procedure? Or a bake sale? Or special fund-raising drives for specific purposes such as the purchase of an organ?

It will be helpful for the group to review the sources of income shown on the Weekly Summary of Receipts, Illustration 19, and add other possible sources.

Some pastors seem to prefer to use a functional breakdown of expenditures into categories such as used by the mythical Spring Hill Church, pages 98-100: (1) Our Ministry to Others; (2) Local Expenses; and (3) Our Ministerial Support. It is readily seen that such a grouping of expenditures does not conform to an acceptable accounting grouping of (1) Assets; (2) Liabilities; (3) Income; and (4) Expenses. The expense items of a particular family are scattered throughout the three categories shown on pages 98-100.

The problem of regrouping all these items so as to form an accounting pattern may be assigned as a class effort to be worked out during class, or as an individual effort to be done as homework. The Chart of Accounts, pages 101-104, may be used as a suggestion.

Accounting for depletion of values to physical assets through recording depreciation should be discussed, including designing appropriate forms and records for reflecting loss of values due to obsolescence.

CHAPTER 9. END-OF-PERIOD REPORTING

The acid test of the effectiveness of the accounting system is whether it affords sufficient interpretative statements quickly, authoritatively, and economically. The format of weekly, monthly, quarterly, and annual statements is subject to a great deal of personal preference. Here, then, is fertile soil for growing ideas and encouraging initiative in every member of the group.

Each of the illustrated reports in this chapter may be questioned as to principal objective and completeness. Does it attempt to show too many facts? Does it portray the data in logical sequence? Does it fail to show enough facts? Is it properly designed for easy interpretation? Is it compatible with other accounting forms and records for purposes of transcribing data?

Since there is such wide variation in practice in church accounting method and procedure, it will be helpful to have each member of the group contribute as many reporting forms as he can obtain to be used in a "class" library. From the accumulation of different styles, the class may design a "standard" format for general use.

Illustration 29 may be used as a group project for demonstrating the way such a progress report can serve to dramatize the variations in spending in relation to the budget.

CHAPTER 10. THE PERIODIC AUDIT

This subject provides an opportunity to point up the neglect of a very critical problem in many churches. Too frequently, churches that handle large sums of money and spend thousands of dollars on various activity programs fail to evaluate their progress and protect their financial resources by a periodic audit. There is continuing need for both an internal audit of finances and functional effectiveness, and for an outside audit by certified accountants.

It has been suggested that a church with an annual budget of $50,000 or more should have an outside audit at least biennially. In most congregations, there are one or more accountants who are available for an internal financial audit on an annual basis. The class may be led into a discussion of the several reasons for conducting the periodic audit as well as the continuous internal audit, by members of the church staff.

A fruitful discussion can be had on the theme of a comprehensive audit of the human resources and program effectiveness of the church. List on a blackboard the different phases of the church program that can profit from an objective evaluation at frequent intervals. How does the church discover latent talent among its membership? What is the church's responsibility for developing its leadership potential? How well is the educational program being conducted? Are there persons with musical talent who are not singing in the choir, or acting as accompanist in church school or other worship groups? How are talent searches conducted? These and many questions will serve to focus attention on the necessity for exploring the congregation for potential leaders and artists.

Index

INDEX